Praise for *Seeking Wisdom*

"Julia Cameron's new book, *Seeking Wisdom,* carries on the author's tradition of magically changing lives, hearts, habits, and attitudes. Julia writes about her own life and about writing and living, and in this six-week guide to contemplation, prayer, and seeking the living presence, Julia does again what she has done since writing *The Artist's Way*: she leads us into the real questions and answers that lie in our path, points to contemplation of the Higher Power in our creative inner lives, and points us to the spiritual approach—prayer, work, writing, and living. She is a master of her craft of giving to others what her inner guides have taught her, and I promise you will come away from reading her new book, as I did, with renewed creative zest and energy, as well as insight into your own spiritual possibilities as a creative person. Get this book—*Seeking Wisdom*; it holds magical wisdom and genuine truth."

—Judy Collins, singer, songwriter, author

"In *Seeking Wisdom,* the prolific Julia Cameron continues her work as a masterful guide, offering a path of creative recovery by asking us to personalize our sense of God through our own intimate practice of prayer. Both grounded and innovative, this book casts writing as praying on the page to everything larger than us. Bring your whole self to the journey of this book and you will touch the eternal link between creativity and spirituality. This book will help you come alive. It will help you play your instrument and sing your song."

—Mark Nepo, author of
The Book of Soul and *Finding Inner Courage*

SEEKING
WISDOM

MEMOIR

Floor Sample: A Creative Memoir

FICTION

Mozart's Ghost

Popcorn: Hollywood Stories

The Dark Room

PLAYS

Public Lives

The Animal in the Trees

Four Roses

Love in the DMZ

Avalon (a musical)

The Medium at Large (a musical)

Magellan (a musical)

POETRY

Prayers for Little Ones

Prayers for the Nature Spirits

The Quiet Animal

This Earth
    (also an album with Tim Wheater)

FEATURE FILM

God's Will (as writer-director)

SEEKING WISDOM

The Spiritual Path to Creative Connection

A SIX-WEEK ARTIST'S WAY PROGRAM

JULIA CAMERON

ST. MARTIN'S
ESSENTIALS

NEW YORK

First published in the United States by St. Martin's Essentials, an imprint of St. Martin's Publishing Group

SEEKING WISDOM. Copyright © 2021 by Julia Cameron. All rights reserved. Printed in Canada. For information, address St. Martin's Publishing Group, 120 Broadway, New York, NY 10271.

www.stmartins.com

The Library of Congress Cataloging-in-Publication Data is available upon request.

ISBN 978-1-250-80937-7 (trade paperback)
ISBN 978-1-250-84763-8 (hardcover)
ISBN 978-1-250-80938-4 (ebook)

Our books may be purchased in bulk for promotional, educational, or business use. Please contact your local bookseller or the Macmillan Corporate and Premium Sales Department at 1-800-221-7945, extension 5442, or by email at MacmillanSpecialMarkets@macmillan.com.

First Edition: 2022

10 9 8 7 6 5 4 3 2 1

To Domenica,
whose prayers light my life

CONTENTS

INTRODUCTION

"Prayer is talking to God," so the adage goes. That's simple enough, and yet for many people, prayer is a difficult subject. "How do I talk to God?" they ask. "God" and "prayer" can be loaded words, often associated with an organized religion that we may or may not have broken from. There are as many definitions of God—and prayer—as there are people to define it. In writing this book, which spanned a cold and snowy New Mexico winter, I wrote, and I prayed—and I talked to my friends and colleagues about prayer.

At the core of our relationship to God is our understanding of God. In the six weeks that follow, we will begin by examining the "God concept" we were raised with. We will explore the possibility that we can convene with a god of our understanding—and then we will experiment with talking to this Higher Power, however we choose to define it.

"Speak to God in your own words," a sage advised me four decades ago, as I was struggling in early sobriety. I was raised Catholic, and had spoken of using a formal prayer and saying it on my knees. The advice to be more

Why must people kneel down to pray?

—L. M. MONTGOMERY,
ANNE OF GREEN GABLES

colloquial found me praying more intimately, and not on my knees.

"Dear God, I'm miserable," I prayed. "I'm depressed, angry, and out of sorts. Please help me." I experienced relief at being so plainspoken. I was speaking as an intimate— even as a lover might speak. I found myself feeling assured God had heard my prayer. I was speaking in my own words, speaking with honesty. I found I presumed God's listening ear. This was, for me, a flier into a prayer that *worked*. No longer content with formal prayers, I began to pray with greater confidence. After all, I was now candidly "talking" to God.

I cannot convey to you the relief I felt, knowing that I was being authentic. Where before I had prayed begrudgingly, "Thy will be done," dreading the worst, I now began to sense God as truly benevolent. As I trusted to God the secrets of my heart, I sensed that God was accepting all of me. No longer tailoring my prayers to please a distant God, I prayed now with greater ease. As I spoke of all of me, I experienced faith. As I trusted, God felt to me to be trustworthy. Praying with candor, I felt God to be welcoming. As I mustered my courage to speak of difficult things, I felt my difficulties diminish. My newly intimate God took a hand in my affairs. As I prayed for guidance, I was guided. A step at a time, I found myself led.

MY OWN STORY

It was 4 a.m. on a Wednesday morning. I woke with a start and reached for the bedside bottle to drink myself back to sleep. Oh, no! The bottle was empty. I had no alcohol to put me back to sleep and without a drink I would lie there, sleepless. I squinted my eyes shut, willing sleep to come, and with sleep, oblivion. For five days I had been drinking around the clock, unable or unwilling to fight the craving for another drink. Without a drink, my consciousness was painful. My husband had left me four days earlier, exclaiming in disgust, "This isn't going to work, Julia."

The "this" was my drinking. He hated my drinking and I hated sobriety. He thought I was an alcoholic and I tried not to drink. I watched him cross the living room, cross the patio, cross the lawn. I watched him climb into his sports car and zoom away from the curb. I watched his car disappear down the roadway.

"This time you've really lost him," my inner voice announced. And then, "You need a drink." I drained the last of a bottle of scotch and phoned the liquor store for more.

"Could you bring me some J&B, some Jose Cuervo, some Stolichnaya?" I asked, careful not to slur. Within fifteen minutes the liquor store fulfilled my request. I thanked the delivery man, tipped him, and poured myself a drink. Had that look on his face been pity? I gulped the drink, not wanting to think about what the man saw: a drunken woman, slurring her thank-yous and pouring herself a drink before he closed the door.

By now it was late morning, early for a normal drinker, late for me. My infant daughter was napping in her crib. My housekeeper viewed me with concern. I took the drink and the drink took another drink. It would go on like this for the better part of a week, until I woke that Wednesday morning to an empty bottle and the chilling realization that the liquor store wouldn't open for hours.

"What can I do?" my brain drummed frantically. "What can I do?"

The answer came to me: call a friend on the East coast. It was later there. Hands shaking, I dialed a number: my friend Claudia. She answered, still sleeping, on the second ring.

"Claudia," I blurted. "What am I going to do?" I thought I was talking about my husband leaving. Claudia

The inner voice is something which cannot be described in words. The time when I learnt to recognize this voice was, I may say, the time when I started praying regularly.

—MAHATMA GANDHI

thought something else. The child of an alcoholic father, she knew about desperate, booze-fueled phone calls.

"I'll call you back," she said, and the phone went dead.

"Oh, my God," I thought frantically, "I've even lost Claudia." Claudia, who had always been so understanding. Claudia, who—

The phone rang. I jumped to answer it. "Claudia?" I asked, eager to hear my friend's warm voice, to be assured we were still friends.

"Julia," a cool voice said. "Here is a number for you to call. I think you need to talk to another alcoholic."

"Claudia!" I exclaimed, offended. "You don't really think I'm an alcoholic?!"

"Well . . ." Claudia said, and that was all.

"All right. I'll call," I told her belligerently.

That was forty-two years ago. As Claudia intuited, I was at my bottom, ready to admit my alcoholism. I needed to talk to another alcoholic. The number she had given me was for a woman named Susan. Susan was an alcoholic.

"I'm an alcoholic and a screenwriter," I told this stranger, desperate to hold on to some prestige.

Susan understood.

"I'm going to call a friend of mine named Edie. She'll want to come talk to you. Can you keep from taking a drink until she gets there?"

"Yes," I said. And so I was launched into sobriety.

I've often thought about the chain of events that fateful day. I *happened* to call Claudia, who *happened* to have a number for Susan. And so, I *happened* to get sober. The chain of events was miraculous. Did I need further proof of a merciful God? When I was ready to surrender, a Higher Power caught me by the hand. This Higher Power was compassionate, merciful. I was saved, rescued, yanked back from the brink. Over time I've come to see—and believe—in a god of mercy. How else to explain my fate?

ON JANUARY 25, 1978, I was advised that if I wanted to stay sober, I should pray. I wanted to stay sober, there was no mistaking that, but *pray*? I'd had sixteen years of Catholic education and I often joked that it was the greased slide to atheism. Prayer was something Catholics did, and something that I did without. I was rebellious; agnostic if not atheist.

"But surely you must believe in *something*!" I was told.

Cornered, I confessed, "Well, I do believe in something. I believe in a line from Dylan Thomas: 'The force that through the green fuse drives the flower.'" Creative energy was what I believed in—*all* that I believed in.

"Great," I was told. One woman announced, "I pray to sunspots." Another chimed in, "I pray to Mick Jagger." Clearly my line from Dylan Thomas fit right in. I could believe in anything.

"As long as it isn't yourself," I was told.

And so, wanting desperately to stay sober, I tried prayer—what I thought of as "secular prayer." I talked to the Universe.

"It's very straightforward," I was counseled. "The day will come when you will have no defense against the first drink. Your defense must come from a Higher Power."

Surely, I thought, enough self-knowledge would be a defense. I knew I was an alcoholic and I knew I couldn't drink.

"Not good enough," I was told. "If you really are an alcoholic, you will have a curious mental blank spot. You will be unable to recall to mind with sufficient clarity the consequences of taking the first drink."

Experienced for a decade with blackout drinking, times when my memory was simply erased, I was ready to believe in "a curious mental blank spot." I thought of it as a sober blackout, and the prospect of its striking me—from out of the blue—terrified me. I could avoid blackouts by not drinking, but how could I avoid "a curious mental blank spot?" It could strike me stone-cold sober. There had to be some defense, some help, some rescue.

"The answer is simple," I was told.

"Simple?"

"Prayer."

"Prayer? I hate prayer. I'm bad at it."

"Pray anyhow."

"But—" I rebelled at the thought.

"But nothing. Ask Him in the morning to give you another day of sobriety. At night, thank Him."

"I suppose I have to get on my knees?" I was sarcastic.

"I do."

Terrified of drinking again, I tried to be open-minded about prayer. While I didn't get on my knees, I did send up telegrams to God.

"Please give me sobriety," and "Thank you for my sobriety today," I managed to mumble. My feeble efforts were rewarded. No curious mental blank spots attacked me. A day at a time, a prayer at a time, I was granted immunity from drinking. Praying daily as instructed, I was struck sober as promised. After years of blackout drinking, this was miraculous.

Sober, I upped the ante. "If it's a choice between sobriety and creativity, I don't know that I choose sobriety," I protested.

"But there is no choice," I was told. "Without sobriety, there will be no creativity."

Still, I was frightened. To me, drinking and writing went together like, well, scotch and soda. But I had to admit something good was afoot. Praying as directed, my tangled drinker's life began to straighten out.

"Try letting the Higher Power write through you," I was directed.

"What if it doesn't want to?" I asked. But I tried it. Like my life, my prose straightened out. I went from a tortured writer's life to a life in which I wrote with in-

If God has given us life, He is capable of any other thing.

—LAILAH GIFTY AKITA

creased ease and joy. I was rewarded with a flow of ideas and words. Freed from my ego's demand that it be brilliant, my writing became straightforward. Increasingly honest, it became more powerful. Words followed words with grace. I went from writing articles to writing entire books. When I prayed for guidance about what to write next, I was led well and carefully, topic to topic. Over time, I amassed a body of work.

As days became months, became years, I came to trust my "Higher Power." Prayer became more natural—a conversation with a supportive Higher Power, not merely a necessity. My rebellious nature was tamed. My writer's— and my drinker's—prayers were answered. I've been sober and productive ever since.

THE ARTIST'S WAY

An early gift of my sobriety was an unexpected calling to teach. "Build with me and do with me what you will," I was told to pray by my newly acquired sober friends. I prayed, but I was afraid to pray, fearing what God might make of me. I wanted to stay a writer. "Help others," I was told, "and God will help you." And so I reached out to another blocked writer. Helping him to write, I myself wrote, and more freely.

I knew that I could help artists become unblocked— and I thought I was helping just a few people, those artists in my inner circle who were struggling to be productive and open as they worked. These early lessons became my book *The Artist's Way*, which, at the time of this writing, has unblocked five million people around the globe. The creative force—my Higher Power—was working through me. It works through me still.

I have been teaching creative unblocking ever since— four decades now. And one of the core concepts of my teaching is that creativity and spirituality are inextricably linked. Creativity is a path to spirituality—and spirituality is a path to creativity. As we deepen our creativity, we deepen our spirituality. As we deepen our spirituality, we deepen our creativity.

This belief grew out of getting sober—and having to believe in *something*. Desperate, and pushed to define what I believed in, I settled on my line from Dylan Thomas. As I relied on this Higher Power—"the force that through the green fuse drives the flower"—it became clear to me that God was the great artist. When we say "creator," it is a literal term for artist—and so I began to believe that if I pursued my artistry, I would be drawn closer to God. If I pursued knowing the creator, I would have more freedom to create. As I allowed the creator to create through me, it became clear to me that I was in fact a co-creator. By forging a new relationship with the Higher Power, I unblocked myself creatively. At the time, it was an unexpected gift of surrendering to living a sober life. It would become the root of my life's work, and a gift I would go on to share with many, many others.

Praying to God in my own words, praying regularly, I came to a different experience of the world. No longer a hostile and forbidding place, it became, instead, benevolent. No longer dreading the future, I came to look forward to it. I prayed, "Thy will be done," coming to trust that God's will was gentle rather than harsh, happy rather than sad, welcoming rather than forbidding.

A word at a time, prayer was leading me to optimism. As I spoke of my secrets, of my dreams and hopes, I heard, "You will be prospered"—and I came to believe it. It was as if when I took a step toward God, God took a step toward me. We drew closer, ever closer, and our proximity bred faith. When I risked disclosure toward God, God disclosed himself to me. I sensed God's presence, and God's nature—all loving. Where previously I believed in

For myself I am an optimist—it does not seem to be much use to be anything else.

—WINSTON S. CHURCHILL

an authoritarian God, I found my God concept altering. I began to sense a God of wonder. Gazing at a full moon, I heard myself breathe, "I love you," addressing God—the moon's maker. I found God in beauty, and beauty was all around me. The willow tree, the maple, the blue spruce—I saw God in nature. The deer, the fox, the bear—his creatures were varied and miraculous. Spotting a raccoon, I marveled at its antic grace. The hawk, the dove, the raven—my spirit took wings as well. I began to pray from gratitude. "Thank you, God, for the sunset. Thank you, God, for the evening star." Addressing God with gratitude, I had a sense of the miraculous. I felt grace. My mood lifted. There was so much to be grateful for—my health, my home, my friends. I could list dozens of reasons to be grateful. My hair, my skin, my limbs. I was grateful to be alive and breathing, grateful to be at prayer.

I found myself feeling a sense of the presence of God. The more I prayed, the stronger the presence felt. I thought of the Carmelite nuns who spend their entire day at prayer. It is often remarked that nuns seem happy, and I began to have a sense of why. I began to sense that conscious contact could yield many things—a sense of well-being chief among them. Mystics report a sense of ecstasy. Humbler than mystics, regular practitioners of prayer report a sense of satisfaction with their lives as they unfold. Pausing throughout their day to say "thy will be done," they feel the comfort of aligning their lives with God's will for them. Happiness is the result.

My teaching taught me that this was not only true for me, but that it was true for other people as well. We are all creative. We can all call on help from the great creator, and we can all connect to the creator by practicing our creativity. I have often noted that creativity is God's gift to us—and using our creativity is our gift back to God. Using our creativity is a valid and powerful path to God, and as we explore and deepen our creativity, we explore and deepen our relationship with a Higher Power—whether we call that God, the force, or sunspots.

As YOU BEGIN your own journey into talking to God, I ask you to experiment with open-mindedness. If the word "God" is uncomfortable for you, do not let that be a block to greater support and connection. After all, a line from Dylan Thomas worked for me. Sunspots worked for my friend. Mick Jagger worked for another. Many of my students have successfully replaced the word "God" with the phrase "Good Orderly Direction." For the purposes of this book, I will use the word "God." Do not let semantics scare you off. We will work on defining a God that works for you, and we will explore the creative art of prayer: a completely individual endeavor.

THE BASIC TOOLS

The basic tools of a creative recovery—those that I, and many others, have used for decades now—have proven to guide me, and my students, without fail. If you have worked with my tools before, you will be familiar with some of them. If you have not, welcome to what I consider "the greased slide to creative unblocking"—a spiritual path to deeper creativity and deeper connection to the divine. Using these tools, you will see positive change in your life. Using these tools, you will feel a sense of empowerment—and an increased connection with a Higher Power. All of us can talk to God. All of us can practice our creativity as a spiritual path. These tools are tried and true. I encourage you to experiment with them for yourself.

MORNING PAGES: THE BEDROCK TOOL
OF A CREATIVE RECOVERY

Morning Pages, the bedrock tool of a creative recovery, have been used by actors, lawyers, writers, directors, bankers . . . no matter one's profession, or whether a person is a "declared" artist or not, people of all stripes have used this tool to expand their creativity, organize their businesses, sort out their personal lives, and yes, talk to God. Morning Pages bring clarity, direction, and productivity to every area of our lives.

So what are Morning Pages? They are three pages of longhand writing about anything. Yes—they must be done in the morning. Morning Pages lay out a track for the day ahead, while "evening" pages reflect on a day that has passed—and that you are now powerless to change. Yes—they really can be about *anything*. They may jump topic to topic to topic. They may be petty, boring, and repetitive. *I'm awake and I'm tired. I'm annoyed about how Sue tried to tell me how to plan my day yesterday. I don't need her plan. I need to follow my own intuition. I need more coffee. I should get my dog groomed. . . .*

Frequently disjointed and seemingly pointless, Morning Pages serve as a kind of "brain drain" that allows you to release the worries, fears, and distractions standing between you and your day. Another way to think of them is like windshield wipers on a car: they clear a path to a day ahead. I have had students tell me many times that Morning Pages allow them to "happen to their day"—instead of having their day happen to them. Morning Pages make us authentic. Morning Pages move us into action. When we begin each day with a practice of honesty, we tend to be more honest in our lives.

Morning Pages are not meant to be high art. They are not meant to be "writing." For writers, it can be tempting to write them well. Don't. Morning Pages are to be

Writing is prayer.
—FRANZ KAFKA

shared with no one—I have had students burn, shred, and hide them—the pages are completely private, for your eyes only. I have often described them as "a room of one's own"—that elusive wish that Virginia Wolfe saw as so valuable, and that many of us do not have. Morning Pages are a private place to vent, think, and dream. They are a receptacle for whatever stands between you and your day. Don't worry about forgetting the insights they bring up—like a tough-love friend, the pages are likely to bring issues up again and again until you have resolved those issues in your life.

I am often asked if it is okay to have coffee before the pages. My answer is that I would never stand between someone and their morning coffee. Most people have coffee as they write. I often brew a pot the night before, and have cold coffee each morning. If this sounds too fanatical, make your coffee in the morning—just don't spend forty-five minutes brewing the perfect cup. It is important to get to the pages as quickly as possible after waking. Bernice Hill, a Jungian analyst and author, told me of Jung's belief that we have forty-five minutes after waking before our defenses are in place. These first forty-five minutes are the best time to do Morning Pages.

Another common question comes from those with a meditation practice. Which comes first, MPs or meditation? I say Morning Pages. Morning Pages propel us into action. They lay out in front of us what we are wondering and worrying about. Meditation runs the risk of allowing the "cloud thoughts" to pass us by—and remain un-acted upon. Practitioners tell me that when they meditate after doing Morning Pages, their insights are clearer and they come away both more serene and more proactive. Morning Pages set the stage for productive meditation: the clarity gained from writing allows for clarity in the communion with the divine.

When I teach a live course and open the room up to Q&A, it is astounding—to me and to the class—how often the answer to a question is "Do Morning Pages." When we are seeking, they lead us. When we are grieving, they soothe us. When we are angry, they listen. When we are anxious, they help us focus. When we are confused, they help us sort. Our priorities float to the surface. Morning Pages push us into action. Try doing Morning Pages. They will lead you to the guidance you seek.

◄ **TRY THIS** ►

For the duration of this course, and hopefully much longer, set your alarm for thirty minutes early. Write three pages—that's three single sides of eight and a half by eleven-inch paper, not six pages!—about anything and everything that pops into your head. Don't judge them. There is no wrong way to do Morning Pages. Just keep your hand moving across the page. At the end of three pages, stop. The pages will change you.

ARTIST DATES: THE PLAY OF IDEAS

The second tool in a creative recovery is something that I call the Artist Date. The Artist Date is a once-a-week, solo adventure that you take just for fun. Think of it as "assigned play." It is during Artist Dates that I often experience synchronicity—the phenomenon of uncanny good luck or coincidence—and feel a sense of connection to God. My students report that Artist Dates bring them inspiration, joy, and peace. They find themselves befriending themselves. It is a truly empowering experience to treat yourself to pure, whimsical fun.

The Artist Date has two parts: "artist" and "date." Our inner artist is a youngster, and the adventure should be something that delights you. Think mystery over mastery, play over virtue. A trip to a children's bookstore, an afternoon at the beach, an outing to a new restaurant, a concert or a play or a movie that's outside your usual scope—anything that sounds fun and frivolous to you will do the trick.

One of my favorite Artist Dates is to visit a pet store with a large bunny named George. The owner allows me to visit George, and my time communing with him brings me a sense of expansion and delight. Do not underestimate how satisfying a simple adventure can feel. The date need not be expensive; often our inner artist, like an inner child, craves time more than money. The act of taking a conscious break with no agenda except for pure delight may feel radical in our culture of constantly being "on." It is. As artists, we are rewarded greatly for taking time out to be festive.

The second part—"date"—informs how you plan this event. Schedule it ahead of time, and allow yourself to look forward to it. This date need only be an hour or two per week for the rewards to be immense.

I often think of Morning Pages and Artist Dates as a two-way radio kit. With the Morning Pages, you are "sending"—*This is what I like, this is what I don't like, this is what I want more of, this is what I want less of.* With the Artist Date you are flipping the dial over to "receive." You are going out into the world on an adventure just for fun and for you—and you can expect to receive guidance, inspiration, and a sense of gentle companionship.

I have had many students report that they felt a sense of a benevolent Higher Power on their Artist Dates—and it is no wonder. When we take this seemingly frivolous adventure, we tap into something larger than ourselves.

The miracle is not to walk on water. The miracle is to walk on the green earth, dwelling deeply in the present moment and feeling truly alive.

—THICH NHAT HANH

The very act of taking our inner artist on a date triggers synchronicity in our lives. We find ourselves in the right place at the same time. We find what we need for a project exactly when and where we weren't looking for it. We stumble upon help and "lucky breaks." Our synchronicity increases manyfold when we take the time out for our Artist Dates. I have heard tell from many, many students that what appeared on the surface to be wasted time turned out to be a shortcut to ideas, solutions, and a sense of well-being.

"It's hard to get myself out the door," a student of mine reports, "but I get such a bang for my buck on my Artist Dates. It never fails. I always come back more enlightened—and more lighthearted. The dates make me a better, more inspired, and more productive artist. And yes—when I am taking regular Artist Dates, my luck definitely increases."

When I teach a large group of students, it is easy to get them on board with doing the "work" of Morning Pages. It is harder to get them to try the "play" of Artist Dates. I invite you to resist your resistance, and do them anyway.

◄ **TRY THIS** ►

Once weekly, take yourself on an Artist Date. Choose an adventure that sounds fun to you, plan it ahead of time, and protect it like you would any important appointment. Make a promise to your inner artist—and keep it. Allow your inner artist to lead you. Allow yourself to listen to their wishes and demands. This solo adventure in pure fun and play will bring surprising insights. Be open to what your artist wants to share with you—and to what you may learn.

(cont'd)

Fill in the following:

It would be fun to . . .

It would be fun to . . .

It would be fun to . . .

It would be fun to . . .

It would be fun to . . .

It would be fun to . . .

It would be fun to . . .

It would be fun to . . .

It would be fun to . . .

It would be fun to . . .

The list you have just completed above is a great resource for potential Artist Dates.

WALKS: A STEP INTO EMPOWERMENT

The third tool of a creative recovery, and one that is as old as the practice of prayer, is walking. For centuries, spiritual seekers have walked—on quests, on pilgrimages, through labyrinths. Artists have long had a practice of walking. Walking stretches not only your legs, but your mind and spirit as well. Writer Brenda Ueland famously said, "I have found that a five- or six-mile walk helps. And you must do it alone and every day." A five- or six-mile walk certainly does help. But if you don't have the time or stamina, a shorter walk can still provide great insight.

Walk as if you are kissing the Earth with your feet.

—THICH NHAT HANH

Twice weekly, you will take a solo, twenty-minute walk. That means no cell phone, no dog, no headphones, no friends. We are creating the opportunity for you to commune with your own thoughts—and your own creator. Walking has long been a connector to the divine. Silent walking has been used by practitioners on all spiritual paths—and the word "path" is significant here. Walking has long been used as a way to talk to God.

I sometimes walk out with a question, and when I do, I find I return with an answer. I sometimes walk, and just listen. I sometimes walk and talk to God, airing my grievances and expressing my gratitude. There isn't a wrong way to take a walk. Simply lace up your shoes and walk for twenty minutes. Allow yourself to connect to the world around you—and the creator who created it.

◄ TRY THIS ►

Twice a week, take yourself alone on a twenty-minute walk. You may walk out with a question, or you may not. Insights will bubble up as you walk. Notice the great creator's hand in the world around you. You are likely to feel a little closer to this creator at the end of your walk than you did at the beginning.

WRITING OUT GUIDANCE: LISTENING TO THE DIVINE

The fourth tool is a tool I began using intuitively, and have come to consciously depend on in my daily life: writing out guidance. When I got sober, and brought a new kind of prayer into my life, I craved some record of the guidance I was receiving. I began to pray on the page. "Please guide me about X," I would pray, listening then for a response, and then writing out what I "heard."

Prayer began to be a dialogue, not a monologue. It was a conversation with me talking to God, and God talking back to me. As I experimented with this practice, I found that what I "heard" back would prove itself to be gentle, accurate, and useful. This is one of the main ways I talk to God to this day.

Outside my windows, the mountains loom high, their peaks snowy. At twilight they glow rainbow-hued, reflecting the setting sun. Today the snowy peaks are apricot. The western sky is vivid rouge. "What shall I write about?" I pose the question to the mountains. "Write about guidance," I hear back. And so I will write about guidance, a Q & A process by which I lead my life.

"What should I do about X?" I ask, and I listen for a response. Pen in hand, pen to the page, I "hear" a reply. I jot down what I hear. Very often, the answers are simple, simpler than I would have thought. For example, I asked for guidance about my ex-husband. Forty years after our divorce, I felt I still loved him and that bothered me. Shouldn't I be over him by now?

"What about still loving X," I wrote. "What should I do?"

"Just love him," I heard back, simple advice that untangled my heart.

"But shouldn't I be over him? I'm ashamed that I still love him," I asked further.

"Love is eternal," the guidance came back. One more time, simple advice. Put simply, "Drop the rock. You love who you love. No need for shame. No need to get 'over' love."

My relief at receiving this guidance was palpable. What to me had been a complicated issue was revealed to be simple. I was directed to follow my heart and when I did, my complications dropped away. Guidance was good on affairs of the heart, I concluded, relieved. But what of more secular matters?

I had promised a book to my beloved publisher who had left "our" press after twenty-seven years. "I'll follow you to your new press," I told him. But our old press had a right to see the book first. I hoped—even expected—that they would reject it. Instead, they loved it. They offered me a hefty advance. What to do? On the one hand I had my promise and on the other I had all that money. Conflicted, I took to the page for guidance.

"What should I do?" I asked.

"Keep your promise," I was told.

"But the money?" I asked.

"Keep your promise," I was told again.

"The money?" I protested.

"Keep your promise," the guidance insisted again.

Reminding myself that guidance had a track record of being right, I decided to keep my promise—money be damned. I turned down the offer from my old press and followed my heart to the new. Would my publisher like the book? I sent him the book and waited on pins and needles for his reaction.

Five long days afterward, his answer came: "I love it."

So now I had a new book deal with an old friend. I reflected that he had always been a muse for me. Our relationship would continue to grow. At our new press, I had a future. At our old press I had a past—and no muse, no matter how much money was offered. The more I mulled on the advice guidance had offered me, the wiser and better it seemed: simple, direct, ethical—"Keep your promise."

On matters large and small, secular or romantic, guidance proved itself reliable over and over again. I asked for help about my writing and was told, "Write about X"—and a topic would be suggested. Like the mountains outside my windows, guidance was always there.

"You are led carefully and well," I was repeatedly assured. Upon reflection, I thought simply, "This is true."

I still use this practice daily. I will refer to myself as

Any concern too small to be turned into a prayer is too small to be made into a burden.

—CORRIE TEN BOOM

LJ—"Little Julie"—and then pose a question. I will listen back for the answer, and then write the response. For example:

LJ: What do they need to know about talking to God?
A: That everyone has a direct line to the Great Creator.

I have learned to listen to my guidance almost constantly, and over many years of taking this guidance, I have come to trust it completely. I may not always believe it in the moment—my human mind may say, "But—?" or "What if—?"—but it has always proven itself to be steady and useful. What we "hear" back will often be surprisingly simple and straightforward. Allow yourself to experiment with this tool whenever you have a question. A sense of support and companionship is likely to be the result.

Prayer is an education.

—FYODOR DOSTOEVSKY

"But Julia," I am sometimes asked, "What if it's just your imagination that your prayers are answered?"

I reply, "If it's just my imagination, it's still good, and my imagination is far wiser than I have thought."

As I developed this practice for myself, I was interested by what I was hearing, and so, praying for guidance to a wise God, I listened carefully. I found my guidance to be warm and reassuring. "There is no error in your path," I was told. "You are led carefully and well." Thus reassured, I found myself able to take risks. When first challenged to risk, I caught myself thinking, "I can't do that." When further prayer led to further reassurance, I thought, "Well, maybe I could try that." And then, "I think I will." My prayers after that were prayers of gratitude. I had risked, and the risk had paid off.

Praying on the page, for "What shall I do next?" I "heard": "You will be writing radiant songs." I was dubious at best. I had been raised as the non-musical one in a hugely musical family. "I'm forty-five years old. If I were the least bit musical I would know it," my thinking ran. But the guidance persisted.

"You will be writing radiant songs."

Two weeks later, seated on a rock by a Rocky Mountain stream, I heard my first song. It was indeed radiant.

As I became accustomed to praying on the page, I became accustomed to guidance giving me a peek ahead. I perhaps didn't know what lay ahead, but guidance did. "Much goodness lies ahead for you," I was told. And, tutored by prayer and optimism, I came to believe it.

◄ TRY THIS ►

Once a day, and more often if you wish, take to the page with whatever is on your mind. Write out a question—any question that you have—listen, and write out what comes back. You may wish to do this right after finishing Morning Pages. You may wish to do as I do—creating your own version of "LJ" for "Little Julie." The point is to be willing to ask, and then be open to receiving. The answers that you hear may surprise you.

WEEK ONE

GOD
CONCEPT

In order to pursue a working relationship with God, we must first examine our own "God concept." In our early attempts to talk to God, we may sense the god we were raised with looming over us, clouding a sense that we have a direct line to a supportive force. For myself, I had to move past sixteen years of Catholic upbringing—by examining my god concept and ultimately creating a new one. I will share tools that I, and my many students, have used to create a god concept that works. I will share my own practice of talking to God, which is considerably more casual than it once was, as well as the practices of my friends.

This week will guide you to explore your own God concept—and to create the god you would *like* to talk to.

GOD CONCEPT

We all know the story.

It's a beautiful day in paradise. All is tranquil and joyous. Then Eve, uppity Eve, plucks an apple from a forbidden tree. She hands the apple to Adam and says, "Sweetheart. Take a bite." Adam, a hopeless codependent, does as he is told. Suddenly the skies part and a booming voice declares, "How dare you? I told you not to eat from that tree! From now on you will bear your children in pain and suffering. In fact, the two of you won't even get along!" And so mankind was doomed to suffer. And suffer we still do!

Now imagine that we learned a different story. Once

again, it's a beautiful day in paradise. Once again, Eve plucks the apple and offers it to Adam for a delicious bite. Then what happens? The skies part and a booming voice declares, "Far out. Took you long enough! I made that apple red for a reason! Enjoy it. For that matter, enjoy each other. All is well."

From story number one, we learn that we have a jealous, punishing God, a God who wants us to know our (lowly) place. From story number two, we learn we have a loving God who encourages us to reach higher, ever higher. If we reach out in prayer to God number one, we do so with fear and trepidation. We grovel as we pray, groveling required. God number two, our loving God, welcomes our prayers, no groveling required.

How many of us still believe in God number one? Is it any wonder so many of us avoid prayer, not wanting to draw God's attention to ourselves? At best, we rebel and withdraw from prayer entirely. After all, we conceive of God as a stern parent. Concerned that we must pray "right," we do not pray at all. We keep our dreams to ourselves.

Imagine now that we have a loving God. How differently we would behave. Assured of their loving reception, our prayers would become conversational, even eager. Knowing God to be benevolent, we would welcome God's attention. Knowing that God is encouraging, we would dare to reveal our dreams. With God's support, we would reach ever higher, expanding to our largest, greatest self. Loving God, we would come to love ourselves. We would come to believe not in original sin but in original blessing.

So how do we exchange our punishing God for a God of love? Musician Michael Reade has this to offer: "I draw inspiration from the earth and the sky. I play piano, drums and flute and I am inspired by what I call 'Eco-Soul.' 'Eco' for the earth and 'Soul' for each of us. It's beautiful to

When you reach the end of what you should know, you will be at the beginning of what you should sense.

—KAHLIL GIBRAN

go through the seasons noting the changes." The natural world is our great teacher, Michael notes. Appreciating nature, he feels "music bubbling up." Music itself is a source of prayerful inspiration for many of us. Composer Tim Wheater draws his musical inspiration from the "song-lines" of Australia. His music, in turn, inspires listeners to appreciate the natural world. *Green Dream*, as one of his albums is named, has a druidic love of nature. Listening to it, I am uplifted. God seems jovial, even merry. Music is indeed a "stairway to heaven," as director Michael Powell called it. For those of us who live in cities and are unable to access nature directly, music is a dependable source of inspiration, moving the listener to higher realms. As composer Johannes Brahms boldly proclaimed, "Straightaway the ideas flow into me, directly from God." For those of us with access to nature, it is easy to see the hand of the creator. Looking past my piñon tree to the mountains beyond, it is easy to visualize the Higher Power, ensconced in their heights, wreathed by clouds.

Speaking for myself, even after forty-two years, my most reliable conception of the divine is still found in the words of poet Dylan Thomas: "The force that through the green fuse drives the flower." That force, powerful and benevolent, strong and yet tender, is a doorway for me to a loving God—and all that we both would create.

TALKING TO GOD: THE HABIT OF PRAYER

Many of us assume that a casual, daily conversation with God is something beyond our reach. For those raised religious, God, after all, is God, and should be addressed "properly." We have many formal prayers, and they are a good starting place, except that they feel so formal. "Our father" may not quite express our relationship to God. Is he a father? And what if we have negative emotions

◄ **TRY THIS** ►

Make a list of at least ten characteristics of the God concept you grew up with. It may look something like this:

1. punishing

2. male

3. all-knowing

4. angry

5. vengeful

6. unforgiving

7. homophobic

8. white

9. shaming

10. judgmental

Now, list ten qualities you would like to have in a God—one that supports your creativity, your most expansive and highest good. For example:

1. welcoming

2. everywhere

3. accepting

4. creative

5. loves to cha-cha

6. loving

7. full of ideas

8. inspirational

9. gentle

10. listening

Many of us have grown up with a toxic God concept. But we are allowed to design the God we choose to talk to. Allow yourself to muse on the page about the kind of God you would like to have as a constant companion. Going forward, allow yourself to talk to that God.

about fatherhood? "God Almighty," we might begin, but that puts a great distance between us and God. "Lord," we might say simply, but that, too, sounds formal. "Dear God," we might at first start, settling on direct address.

God has ears for all of our prayers, however awkward we may feel them to be. God, after all, is all-merciful, and his mercy extends to our feeble attempts at prayer. And so we address God as best suits us. We search for the "right" way to pray, and settle on what feels most comfortable to us. "Dear God," we might pray, reflecting that God is, to us, dear, both close and beloved. Our relationship to God is intimate, and we choose a term that expresses that fact.

In prayer all are equal.

—RUMI

I have found, for myself, "Dear God" to be my best and most suitable form of address, claiming as it does a respectful intimacy. I believe in a listening God, and the term "Dear God" captures God's attention. We have God's ear, so to speak, and now we may enumerate our concerns, addressing God however we choose.

It is Thanksgiving morning. My bedroom window opens onto my courtyard—and at dawn, the window revealed six inches of snow. I pad to my kitchen. Coffee. I live atop a mountain in Santa Fe, with a beautiful view of the Sangre de Cristo mountains. The cost of the view, though, is a drive up a dirt road, which isn't plowed regularly in the winter. My neighbors and I have all decided that the view is worth the price, but on days like today, with snow falling, I begin to worry about my ability to venture out into the world.

I was planning on spending Thanksgiving with my friend Nick and his family, and was due to check in with him at noon. We would decide then about braving the roads to his house. Settled on the love seat, I watched with dismay as more snow fell. We were rapidly accumulating a full foot. The storm was beautiful, but dangerous. In order to be "fine," as my friend Julianna had predicted I would be in making the drive, I would need to be cautious.

"What should I do?" I prayed. An unwelcome answer came to me.

"Call Nick and tell him you are choosing to stay in."

Resentful but obedient, I phoned Nick. When I told him my decision, he sounded relieved. "I'll save you a plateful," he told me. "Only about half of our guests are coming. The rest are stuck." And so, not wanting to be stuck, but craving human companionship, I reached out by phone to my friend Sonia, living in Paris, spending a solo Thanksgiving like myself. No answer at Sonia's. Next I tried my friend Scottie, at her home in Southern California. I knew her to be comfortable in solitude, and as she was only a week into recovery from an oral surgery, I suspected she would be forgoing a Turkey Day feast. Scottie answered her phone with her own dire weather report.

"I'm fogged in. I can't see the boats in the harbor. In fact, I can't see past my patio."

Scottie's solution for her isolation was to light incense, praying for ease and joy. She told me that in the pre-dawn hours she had lit a stick of incense for my writing. I pictured the stream of smoke inviting forward my flow of words, that they might both drift heavenward together.

I hung up the phone and peered out the windows. The mountains were blotted out by the storm. A few intrepid ravens flapped near, but even their raucous caws were muted. Yes, it was a day to be conservative. In the piñon tree, tiny birds took refuge. Its snow-laden branches drooped low, close to my window pane. This year, the tree had held a full harvest of piñon nuts, enough to feed the tiny birds and the ravens both.

Watching the birds pick their way delicately amid the branches, I am struck by their gentle optimism. Snow notwithstanding, they will be fed. An affirmative prayer comes to my mind: "Everything is in divine right order." By "everything," at the moment, I mean the storm. Like the little birds safe among the branches, my little dog Lily, and I myself, are safe. If I allow myself to feel the hush of the snow, I have a quiet sense of the miraculous. Rather than isolated, I feel connected. Jacob, in Idaho, is making mashed potatoes. My daughter Domenica, in Chicago, has made cherry crumble. Emma, in frigid Maine, has baked chocolate cupcakes with her niece, who is wearing a unicorn robe and slippers Emma brought to her from London. My whole far-flung world is feasting, like the little birds.

From Scottie and Julianna, I am tutored to pray for acceptance. Scottie has fog, and Julianna has snow, but her son, driving his Prius, made it in before the storm. When I talk to Julianna briefly, she is quietly happy. She and her son have spent a gentle day watching Turner classics—*Lawrence of Arabia* and *Citizen Kane*. The artistry of the films and the company of her son—like she herself, a poet—have filled her with joy.

"I keep on praying," Julianna tells me, "all the time." And so, faced with the storm, she prayed for acceptance— and later, blessed by her son's appearance, she sent up prayers of gratitude. Her prayers are a constant; a steady stream, "a flow of words."

It's late afternoon and the storm has briefly abated. My view extends to the mountains, which are still blanketed in snow clouds. I pray silently, "Dear God, let me be safe to drive out tomorrow." The break in the storm fills me with optimism. It might indeed be possible. My dirt road holds warmth and melts the snow. We are not plowed, but nature has its ways.

You can cut all the flowers but you cannot keep spring from coming.

—PABLO NERUDA

Now the base of the mountains is clear. The storm may be receding. I can see farther than Scottie on her patio, and I am grateful for the view. I look northeast, across the mountains, toward Idaho, Chicago, and Maine.

"Just checking on you. We're about to eat," Emma phones to tell me. "I'll call you later."

Here, the sky is darkening. In Maine, it is dark. Chicago, perpetually dark in winter, perches by the frigid lake. Jacob sends me photographs of Boise—like Santa Fe, mountainous with snow. In my Morning Pages, I pray for my "beloveds." I ask God to please remember—and bless—everyone I love. My list—God's list—is long, and grows longer. I pray for the living and the dead, for joy, health, peace, and acceptance.

One recent morning, I felt agitated, and I prayed, instead, for personal guidance. I felt guilty, praying, it seemed to me, so selfishly. But when my guidance spoke to me it said, "Don't worry. I have your loved ones in my care. Don't feel the weight of your prayers. Instead, feel lighthearted." There is no limit to what we can ask for God's help with. Ourselves, our beloveds, the people sick and suffering who we will never meet.

I am reminded of Scottie's daily prayer for "ease and joy." I think of Julianna praying on her mountaintop, and Nick, across town, saving me a plate. "Do not doubt my goodness," I have been instructed. And God's goodness is apparent, today of all days. "Be happy, joyous, and free," sober alcoholics are instructed, urged to put behind them their dark and heavy past. "We are not a glum lot," advised AA's cofounder Bill Wilson, whose life was filled with gratitude for his own miraculous reprieve.

And so, faced as I am with enforced human solitude, but with God as my companion, I strive to have a light heart. I find the passing storm beautiful, not merely dangerous, an opportunity for reflection, not merely an inconvenience. I'm grateful for my "flow of words," and I am reassured of their validity as I ask:

LJ: Can I hear guidance about the new book?

I hear, "Prayer is a topic you need to explore. You can write well about it. Do not worry that you are barking up the wrong alley. You will find yourself able to write freely. You are on the right track."

A light dusting of snow covers my portal. Peering out the door, I see Lily's tracks. She goes to the portal's edge, no farther. I call her in, happy for her company. Together, we curl on the love seat, her paws, wet from the snow, smearing my notebook. I tell her that she is writing with me, that together we are not a "glum lot."

Taking my cue from Bill Wilson, I experience a surge of gratitude. After all, I, too have been rescued. There is no wine bottle by my side. Instead, coffee with cinnamon. I take a sip and breathe, "Thank you, God." I am remembering the Thanksgiving before I got sober. I cooked all morning, drinking as I cooked, and then, serving the festive meal, I passed out. Today the memory floats back to me and I sigh it away. Two months later I would be struck sober, praying for divine intervention—a finally self-acknowledged chronic alcoholic in need of spiritual intervention.

"Dear God," I now pray, "show me what to write about prayer." I listen, and I hear: "Keep it simple." And so my advice becomes, "Pray as you are comfortable praying. Pray prayers of gratitude. Pray prayers of petition. Pray formal prayers. Pray in your own words. Pray walking. Pray kneeling. Do what suits you, or what you think suits God."

My friend Robert, a photographer, prays in the dark

room, "making things of beauty." My friend Michael, asked to pray, taps his chest and says, "I hold you in my heart."

My daughter Domenica prays with Morning Pages, with making gingersnaps, with reading with her daughter, who, at seven, has read all—that's all—of the Harry Potter books.

I am a writer and I pray by writing. This book is a prayer. I move my hand across the page, and I listen for "the flow of words," what to write next. I hear a next word, a next thought, and I try to take it down accurately. "Don't be alarmed by what you write," guidance comes to me. And so I write the word "guidance," trusting readers know that, put most simply, "guidance" is shorthand for an answered prayer.

When I talk to Jacob Nordby, a fellow writer, he tells me, "I pray on the page in the morning, and I get answers." We agree that writing is, for both of us, a comfort. He says, "I tell people that Morning Pages are a way to meet your own best friend."

"That," I think to myself, "is a lovely, gentle way to think of God."

My phone rings. It is my friend Ezra, whose name means "help." He is calling from his studio in Florida, working late against a deadline.

"Happy Thanksgiving," he wishes me. He is busy making art for an installation two days out.

"Happy Thanksgiving to you," I wish him back. "So you're praying a piece of art at a time?" Ezra has told me before that his work is guided by prayer.

"Exactly," he says now. "I listen, make a piece, listen, make a piece, listen, make a piece—I'm guided and I'm obedient to the guidance. Do we have a choice?" Ezra chuckles.

Many people don't listen, or don't obey, I think to myself, but to Ezra, I say, "Ez, I'm so proud of you. I pray for you daily for joy. I pray for 'Ezra plus'—meaning your highest creative self."

"I like that!" Ezra exclaims. Across the room from me here in Santa Fe, I have one of his sculptures. It is a circle of wood bisected by a cross. The piece combines eternity and humility. In solid, three-dimensional form, it is a prayer.

"I'm working in a circular space," Ezra tells me next. "The circle, to me, is a sacred form."

"I'm living in a circular space," I think to myself. But Ezra is asking me, "Today, in your solitude, did you write?"

"Without a wine bottle at my elbow," I report. "Just coffee and a large bottle of water."

"So I'm proud of you," Ezra signs off. "You wrote, and wrote well."

The snow in my courtyard blows lightly in the wind. Lily is peaceful, stretched out on the love seat. In a brief call, Julianna reports that she, too, is still snowbound, but happy with her son. Domenica calls in that she and her husband successfully hosted a Thanksgiving feast for his family. I tell her I am proud of her, and she replies that she read her sister-in-law a portion of *The Artist's Way* so I was there, at least in spirit. Readying myself for bed, I take out my journal and read the morning's guidance. "Today your need is solitude. Write. Write now." I'm happy that I obeyed.

◄ **TRY THIS** ►

Reread your newly designed God concept. Keeping in mind this benevolent force, allow yourself to ask for help and guidance. Fill in the following sentences:

(cont'd)

If it weren't so silly, I'd try talking to God about . . .

If it weren't so silly, I'd try talking to God about . . .

If it weren't so silly, I'd try talking to God about . . .

If it weren't so silly, I'd try talking to God about . . .

If it weren't so silly, I'd try talking to God about . . .

If it weren't so selfish, I'd try asking God to . . .

If it weren't so selfish, I'd try asking God to . . .

If it weren't so selfish, I'd try asking God to . . .

If it weren't so selfish, I'd try asking God to . . .

If it weren't so selfish, I'd try asking God to . . .

If it were easy to talk to God, I'd say . . .

If it were easy to talk to God, I'd say . . .

If it were easy to talk to God, I'd say . . .

If it were easy to talk to God, I'd say . . .

If it were easy to talk to God, I'd say . . .

THE INDIVIDUALITY OF
TALKING TO GOD

As I talked to my friends about how they talked to God, I found that there were as many paths to understanding a Higher Power as there were ways of communicating with one. Prayer is both very universal and very individual. And what is prayer, at its core? When we are children, we ask "why" about the questions that have no answers. *Why did the earthquake hurt the people who didn't do anything wrong? Why did my dog run away? Why did my friend get sick?*

And then, there is wishing and hoping—*I wish there hadn't been an accident. I wish my dog would come back home. I wish my friend felt better. I hope a natural disaster doesn't hurt my loved ones. I hope my dog comes home. I hope my friend's surgery goes well.*

We ask why, we wish, we hope—as children, and then later—and at the core of all of these questions is an innate human desire to find an answer where no human power can really give us one. Yes, science may offer us some answers, and our friends have opinions, as we do. But there are also ways in which we have never been able to explain everything, and so, for as long as humans have existed, in one form or another, we have prayed.

CLAD IN DENIM head to toe, painter Barbara McCulloch settled in to a Central American meal at the cozy diner The Red Enchilada.

"This is delicious," she said, sampling her meal, downing a savory bite. "Is that your sopapilla or mine?" she asked.

"We'll share," I told her, slathering honey on a tasty morsel.

"I was raised German Lutheran," she began her remarks on prayer. "After that, I avoided God. My only prayer was glancing in the rearview mirror as I drove, saying 'Please don't let that be a cop.'

"I drank a quart of vodka a night and once, at midnight, I prayed, 'Oh God, help me,' and the next day went for help. I stayed dry for a year and then I drank for three more years—as I said, a quart of vodka a night until my body was gone. I called for help again but didn't feel I deserved to be helped. Instead I prayed, 'Dear God, please give me a heart attack.' And then, when that didn't work, I prayed, 'Please put me in a coma.' I had nothing left, no hope for the future. Finally I prayed, 'Okay, God, you do it. Take my life.' I felt a pink blanket of peace. I thought, 'This is God.' People get what they're missing and this peace was an experience beyond comprehension. I knew it was God."

Sipping her water with lemon, Barbara continued. "I went from very drunk to very spiritual. I knew I couldn't understand God, but I said, 'Okay, God, put it in my path and give me the strength to do it.' I called that my 'walking prayer.'"

Ordering flan for dessert, Barbara went on. "I was open to anything. I opened my book on religions—all branches of Christian religion—and I said, 'God, show me.' I landed on the section on the Augustan Lutheran Church. Its mission was to help others, and I felt called to do the same. And so I prayed, 'God, come to me. Show me who I can help.' Prayer, I realized, was being receptive. I want to be like a garden hose. God comes through me like water. God goes where God wants to go. If I get my ego out of the way, I am open to God and my prayer becomes 'send me where I am needed.'"

TEACHER LAURA WAARVICK slid into a booth at Santa Fe Bar & Grill. She sported oversized hoop earrings and a mustard-yellow sweatshirt emblazoned with "Good Vibes."

The Ego is a veil between humans and God.

—RUMI

She paired the sweatshirt with blue jeans and thigh-high boots. With sparkling rings on her fingers and a delicate gold necklace, she herself embodied "good vibes." Her shoulder-length bob of honey-gold hair swished as she nodded her "hello." She ordered hot water with lemon and a large salad before settling in to talk about prayer. A teacher of gifted children aged kindergarten through sixth grade, she had a warm smile and sparkling blue eyes. Her smile flashed small, even teeth as she launched into her topic with contagious enthusiasm.

"I was never taught to pray as a child," she began. "As a youngster, I had what I call a 'transactional prayer,' asking for gifts from a 'Santa Claus God.' Not 'How can I be of service?' Both sets of grandparents went to church. My dad's parents were Lutheran, super involved, going to church Sunday, Wednesday, Saturday. I remember when I was little, five or six, asking my grandmother, 'Is God a man?' She said, 'Oh, yes.' I said, 'I don't know about that,' and she got mad at me."

Laura's salad arrived and she took a delicate nibble, continuing. "I liked church, the different seasons and songs, but I didn't like getting up early. My parents didn't belong to any organized religion, and even made fun of it—but they definitely believed in something bigger, kindness, and love. But don't talk about prayer. That's private. Meanwhile, my grandmother said she prayed for me.

"As a teenager, I read about Eastern religions, but if it was strict I didn't like it. I read lots of books, wanting a God that was kind and loving. I found Marianne Williamson's books and read several hungrily. I was searching, but I was also drinking, and the alcohol muddled my mind."

Laura paused, trying to sum up a dark period in her life. After a long beat, she explained, "I had strong intuition which I didn't follow when I was drinking. When I got sober, I listened to guidance again. The longer I'm sober, the more I listen—and when I don't, I regret it."

And yet, turning sober, Laura was reluctant to pray. "I fought prayer at first. Then I started meditating and things became much more clear." Still, it took a crisis to propel her fully into prayer. At one time happily married, her husband eventually became mentally ill. He turned mean and abusive. Feeling torn between loyalty to her husband and loyalty to herself, Laura turned to prayer. That is when the concept of God began to gel.

"God is a loving presence if you want to access it. It loves us no matter what. It's soft, still, quiet. It tells us everything is okay. It has been okay. It will be okay."

Laura pushed aside her salad plate to concentrate more fully. She continued, "God is a source that has always been there. Not born. Won't die. God is in everything and everywhere. God is bigger than I can comprehend."

But with her newfound God-consciousness, Laura still experienced despair. "When my husband got ill, I got angry at God. Why take away my great love? There, but gone? If I ever meet God face to face, I will ask, 'Why?' Maybe someday I'll understand."

But for now, Laura said, she lived with unresolved grief. And for comfort, she found prayer. "I talk to God all day long. And then I listen. It's better to listen than try to figure it out. Why such loneliness? Why so empty? Maybe it's for me to know to 'just do the next right thing.' Call a friend. Take a bath. Go to the gym. Just accept what is, no deep questions."

Taking a final sip of her lemon water, Laura summed up her current consciousness. "I have a running conversation with God. 'What next? What's the best thing?' I listen for an intuitive answer. I get guided.

"Let me tell you a story. I regularly went to Starbucks, and one day, there was a new barista. I thought, 'Wow. He's cute.' And then I heard this loud voice inside me say, 'No. Stay away.' I listened to the voice and stayed away, no matter how cute he was. Well, he murdered his

There is a crack in everything. That's how the light gets in.

—LEONARD COHEN

wife and two small children. He chopped them up and buried them in a marsh. So I say now with certainty, 'Something protects us if we listen.'"

BEARDED AND WELL-BARBERED, Nick Kapustinsky hid his dark locks under a baseball cap emblazoned with a fleur-de-lis. He wore a green tweed sweater and khaki pants, well-worn cowboy boots and a jaunty air. He was prepared to talk about his prayer life, although his demeanor was quite secular, his black Irish good looks enlivened by humor. His flashing blue eyes filled with mischief. Settling in at our favored New Mexican dive, The Red Enchilada, Nick nestled into a bright turquoise booth under the watchful eyes of a primitive mural of a peasant woman bearing a basket of plantains.

"Shall we?" he asked rhetorically as he launched into a history of his prayer life. "When I was very young, I had a clear conception of a Higher Power that could speak to me. It was a conversation, never asking for something like Santa Claus, but having realized a depression and isolation, I sought a voice outside myself filled with reason and love. I would consult the voice for wisdom."

Nick paused, ordering a bowl of posole with red chili and onions. He was, after all, a native New Mexican. He continued, "I was fascinated by the church, but by the time I went to Catholic school, prayer was something very different that I rejected. At the start of each class, we would say a prayer and then be asked for any intentions. The intentions were for petty and selfish things, and they turned me against prayer. Leviticus would turn anyone atheist, reading the Bible. I was rebellious in a good way as a young person. I saw the damage of organized religion."

Nick spooned onions into his bowl of posole, tasted it, and added more. He went on, "I saw prayer as a very facile thing. I was very sensitive to injustice. I wanted people to act, not wish for things. It seemed to me prayer was a way to absolve their conscience without action. It made me angry."

Sipping a Coca-Cola, Nick continued. "Growing up, my father was a particle physicist. Initially, I grew up thinking of the universe with God seeming an absurdity, a relative impossibility. I was a confident young atheist with Nietzsche as my sidekick. But then I remember my father saying to me, 'Nick, there are things in the universe that defy logic. It's important to be open.' I wasn't at the point of praying, but I found in the Irish Catholic community of my father people who met prayer with action. This changed my tune on religion. If it helped people—okay."

Nick's eyes darted upward to the right, praying, per-haps, to be articulate. He went on, thoughtfully. "Now, when I think about prayer, I think of what I was taught: 'energy can neither be created nor destroyed, but it can be manipulated and shared by many means.' So, prayer is energy focused for the good. It is active, not facile. When practiced, prayer can direct energy. When I pray, I am necessarily saying, 'I'm not in charge.' Prayer is an act of humility and that in and of itself is valuable. It is an act of subsuming my own ego. My will and my ego are not the first. I hope to connect with positive energy based on love—that I hope to share. I hope to direct energy in certain ways. If a friend is having trouble, I pray for the resolution of that issue. I try to leave my ego behind. I don't seek to direct the answer, simply that it be resolved."

Nick smiled, ladling posole to his mouth. It's very good posole, and he would take a container of it home to Meg, his sick girlfriend. "Medicine," he explained. A last sprinkling of onions went into the bowl. "Great," Nick pronounced the result. Then he turned to his concluding thoughts.

"I was very reluctant to get on my knees," he con-

Choose to be optimistic, it feels better.

—DALAI LAMA XIV

fessed. "Then I was asked, 'Do you seek humility?' Now, the first thing I do when I wake is get on my knees. Then I meditate, breathing in my anxieties and the sharp points of ego; breathing out to push them out. I do this for five to twenty minutes, until I'm in a centered space. Then I turn to active prayer. 'Relieve me of the bondage of self.' I move energy toward people who require more than most. I do this with intention, not irony. Finally, I ask, 'What actions can I take?' I write down a list for the day. At the very end of my routine, I write—free write. It squares me away for the day. It gives definition to the person I will be. It allows me to speak freely to the same universe as when I was a child."

Nick set down his spoon, hefted his Coca-Cola, and took a long sip. "Prayer? It's a personal conversation."

◄ TRY THIS ►

Take an hour and spend it in silence. For the first thirty minutes, you will write a letter to the benevolent god of your understanding. Allow yourself to talk about anything and everything. This is, remember, a helpful and listening god, whose dreams for you are even bigger than your dreams for yourself.

For the second thirty minutes, write a letter to yourself *from* your god. Allow yourself to listen and receive. Keep moving your hand across the page and let this force talk to you. I have found this exercise to be encouraging, hopeful, and emotional. Allow yourself to reflect on what you learned. Did your Higher Power make suggestions that you could incorporate into your life? This practice is a good one to turn to whenever you are feeling in need of guidance. As you practice talking to—and listening to—a supportive God, you will find talking to God naturally becomes a more frequent and automatic part of your life.

RECLAIMING THE MAGIC OF CHILDHOOD

Children are naturally trusting, naturally accepting. We may look at our own childhood to remember a more effortless faith, or we may look at the children in our lives to witness this innocent trust. As we mature, many of us tend to move away from such unquestioning openness, but we can all return to the magic of childhood as we unlearn the toxic lessons most of us have absorbed around the concept of God.

Victoria, director and actor, should add to her credits "equestrienne." She spoke on prayer from Kelly's on 41, an equestrian center where she kept her large black and white pony, Balloo. She had enjoyed an early morning ride and grooming session. "He was wonderful, but he's shedding. I'm covered with black and white pony fur." She laughed with delight. Her pony was now blanketed and satisfied, having been stabled in his box stall and given treats.

"He makes a snuffling sound when he's pleased," she explained. "Although I do think he'd like still more treats."

Petite and fit, Victoria said she wore "layers and layers. Winter gear. A plump coat over a sweatshirt and houndstooth britches." The barn was thirty-three degrees, warmer than usual, so her layers kept her "snug." Striding the rows of box stalls, pausing to pet velvety muzzles, Victoria headed for the arena.

"I pace and pray," she explained, one ear cocked for guidance. Pausing to pet a puffy coated barn cat, she began her story.

"Oh, yes, I prayed when I was little. Although my prayers were more immediate—'thought beams.' I would close my eyes and think, 'Oh, God.' My prayer didn't have to be 'our father' or the 'serenity prayer.' It was more like, 'Wow, God!' 'Oh, God!' twirling under the night sky. I always felt connected. It wasn't just at bed time."

Victoria stepped into the loam of the arena, continuing, "In first grade, I began experimenting with different ways to pray, opening up to different types of prayer. I remember one time distinctly. I was praying prayers of gratitude, blessing me, my family, my animals, then the generations before ours, my grandparents, and their families and friends. I prayed to angels, then guiding angels, and suddenly there was a rush of light across the ceiling. I thought, 'Wow. I better be careful about that prayer.' But I felt heard and connected."

Victoria stepped over a pole, walking the full length of the arena. She recalled, "Not only did I feel I had an immediate connection, I felt free. My prayers weren't formal. I felt I had an actual relationship with a power of my own understanding."

Victoria paused, gathering her thoughts. After a moment, she went on, explaining carefully her childhood experience. "I prayed and I found I got guidance from the same source. I reached out and got fairly immediate feedback. Whatever I felt I 'thought to,' I got nudges from it back. It didn't feel quite one-sided. From early on, prayer was a conversation. It was an interaction. It was connected—me and God."

In the silence of the heart God speaks.

—MOTHER TERESA

Victoria stopped to roll another pole to one side. She continued, "Maybe it was because prayer wasn't spelled out formally—'This is prayer. This is meditation.' For me it was call and answer. An exchange. From the time I was really little, what I saw in nature was more than physical. The wind, the night sky with all its stars, feeling myself planted with feet on the ground, I felt a part of something much bigger. I didn't have a personification or embodiment of God. To me it was a creative force to which I was connected. I was witnessing all the good in life."

As she recalled it, Victoria's connection to God was natural and immediate. Only as she grew older did she learn of a God that was more distant, a God whose connection had to be earned. Instead of being intrinsically joined, this God required that a soul be "good enough."

Exposed to her father's Catholicism, Victoria found herself feeling about prayer that she wasn't doing it right. She wasn't, in the eyes of the church, good enough. She found herself concerned with "shoulds." Prayer and meditation became more formal—focus on a flame, on her breath, on a posture. She felt a great deal of sadness around her father and his Catholicism. While she never felt he wanted her to be a Catholic, she felt he expected her to inherently know what Catholicism meant. Hardest of all, she found herself dealing with a different God— one that was "outside of creation, further away," a God that ran counter to her native feeling of connection. "This God 'of outside' cares—or doesn't care—about its beings or creations."

Victoria paused in her steps. She wanted to explain clearly, "I believed we all came from a divine spark. I had a hard time feeling that we had to earn it. To me, the connection was unconditional. Then to be told it was conditional—why would something so mighty be so limited?"

Victoria resumed her pace. She took a few steps, then paused again. She was remembering that her early exposure to Catholicism had centered on masses at Christmas and Easter. "I didn't understand the focus on suffering. It ran counter to my natural spiritual path that focused on the right of being alive."

Victoria stomped her feet. She wore warm boots but thirty-three degrees was still cold. She resumed her walk with a change of memory. If her father gave her a dark vision of Catholicism, her mother gave her permission to explore multiple spiritual paths. While her mother, like her father, had been raised Catholic, she had set the church aside as she pursued a spiritual path of her own devising. Victoria remembered, "On our bookshelf, we had a book on African Gods, a book on Goddess religion, a children's bible, a book on Greek mythology. I learned that there were many spiritual paths, that each culture had a story, a differing story, of the creation of the world—and a differing conception of a Higher Power."

Victoria resumed her walk. "My mom had a spiritual practice that seemed to be not connected to a church. She prayed when driving. She had a God jar. She prayed through writing. She directly asked for guidance. I do remember lighting candles for folks that had passed away. She gave me a road map to find ways to be close to God— including religion and church, or not."

I never made one of my discoveries through the process of rational thinking.

—ALBERT EINSTEIN

Taking her cue from her mother, Victoria spent her teen and college years experimenting with written prayer and affirmative prayer. As she recalled, "My big questions were about God's will and my will. I asked, 'Do I get to be happy? To do the things that bring me joy?'" Her questions demanded further answers.

At age twenty-three, Victoria enrolled herself in what she now called "prayer boot camp." "Searching for answers, I became willing to explore different God concepts. I tried things. The serenity prayer. A God jar. Sitting silently. Focusing on the breath to see what happens. My communication with God came back to being a conversation.

"My God has a sense of humor. Like the synchronicity of feeling anxious and then immediately seeing a billboard that says 'Relax. We've got this.' I experimented with how to build prayer into my day. I often reach for prayer when I'm in fear or struggling. Let me add, on airplanes. I say a formal prayer. Then I let go, breathe, and hope."

Rounding the far end of the long arena, Victoria turned

to the now. She related her daily practice. "Formal prayers didn't sit right in my mouth. Nowadays, I set my alarm absurdly early, before my husband or my kiddo. I often get guidance even before I get to the page. Then I do my Morning Pages and pour out all the clutter. Then I get more flashes of guidance. Then I sit and pray to turn my will and my life over to the Great Creator. I ask for guidance, and I sit and listen."

Victoria stopped her walk, wanting to focus on precisely how she prayed, however idiosyncratic. She continued, "Then it's time for my husband and my child. I drive my daughter to school and as I enter the car, I take a deep breath, say the serenity prayer. That gives me a moment of grace. Other times I walk my daughter to school and I pray as I walk. I count the birds. I focus on what my daughter has to say. I drop her off. Then I focus on what's next in my day. I ask God to go before me. If I happen to have a concern about money, about a difficult conversation, or work situation, or a challenging personality, I take a beat, take a breath, and say, 'Okay, God, you go first.' Then I walk through the door."

Victoria picked up her pace. She was back at the viewing room where the puffy-coated cat, Jill, launched herself into her arms. Next came a greeting from Cash, a little bay pony, and then from Jaspar, a tri-colored Tennessee Walker. Victoria stopped at each stall, petting each velvet nose. Paused finally at Baloo's stall, she rounded up a last thought.

"I think over the years my God concept has grown a little fuller. My God is big enough that I'm not going to be abandoned if I have difficult emotions, fear or anger. My God takes me precisely as I am." It seems that Veronica has recaptured the intuitive sense she had as a child—and returned to a God who is available, safe, and accepting.

I have so much to do that I shall spend the first three hours in prayer.

—MARTIN LUTHER

> ## ◄ TRY THIS ►
>
> Children are open. They are uncensored and nonjudg-mental. Their emotions come and go freely, and they make no effort to stuff them. No matter our age, we can reclaim the magic of childhood, and believe that our God is large enough and expansive enough to accept all parts of us. Fill in the following sentences:
>
> As a child, I thought God was . . .
>
> An experience I had as a child that felt like God was . . .
>
> A childhood experience that made me question my God was . . .
>
> If God had no limits, I'd . . .
>
> The difference between myself now and myself as a child is . . .

GOD AS LISTENER

It's Thursday night and The Red Enchilada is nearly empty. I place my order: a tamale plate with red and green chili (Christmas) plus a sopapilla. I'm dining with-out Nick this evening. He has "stuff to catch up on," and so I am eating solo, appreciating the quiet in the cafe. My years of taking Artist Dates have made me comfortable in my own company.

Miranda, the young waitress, is a welcoming presence. Her long black hair is piled atop her head. Her long black eyelashes sweep her cheekbones. She is pretty and petite. Taking advantage of the quiet in the cafe, she perches at my booth.

I am so far from being a pessimist . . . on the contrary, in spite of my scars, I am tickled to death at life.

—EUGENE O'NEILL

"What are you writing?" she asks.

"A book on prayer," I tell her.

"I pray," she volunteers. "I pray when I need help, or just when I need someone to listen to me. I grew up praying, and I pray still, age twenty. Growing up, we prayed at meals and at bedtime. Now, I pray throughout the day. My siblings pray, too, but we each pray differently. It's an individual thing. We each pray as we need to. Do you pray?" Miranda asks me.

"Yes," I answer. "In the mornings I write three pages, and then I pray throughout the day. Like when I'm driving, and I say, 'Dear God, please get me home safely.'"

"Ah, yes," Miranda breathes. She, too, prays for safety. "I think I pray because I need to know someone is listening."

"Otherwise it's lonely?" I ask her.

"Yes."

"So your God is a listener?"

"Yes."

God is for Miranda a constant companion, a friend. Talking about God, her tiny face relaxes. Her manner softens and she is eager to talk further.

"There was a time," she says, "when I didn't pray. When my mother got divorced. But I found I missed it, and so I began to pray again. My family is Christian, and so we had formal prayers to say. But I had my own prayers, talking to God."

A bevy of customers enters the cafe. Miranda gets to her feet, rushing to welcome them. She hands them all menus. While they study them, my tamale plate arrives, piping hot. The green chili is particularly delicious. I take tiny forkfuls, waiting for my meal to cool. Miranda stops again at my booth.

"How many books have you written?" she asks.

"Forty," I tell her. "One a year."

"I'd never have the patience," she says.

"And I'd never have the patience to do what you do," I tell her. The new customers are boisterous, ordering in a tumult of voices. I signal for the check, wondering, as I pay it, if Miranda is, even now, praying.

CHECK IN

How many days this week did you do your Morning Pages? Seven out of seven, we hope!

Did you take an Artist Date? What was it? Did you feel an increased connection to your Higher Power during the date? Afterward?

Did you take your walks? What insights bubbled to the fore?

Did you try asking for guidance in writing, and then listening to the answer? What guidance did you receive? Did you try applying it? What surprised you?

WEEK TWO

PRAYERS
OF
PETITION

This week we will be experimenting with the first of three types of prayer: the prayer of petition. Prayers of petition may be the first thing we think of when we think of prayer. It is the act of petitioning God, asking for something we want or need. Sometimes it is asking for guidance, as if from a wise elder. *Please help me know how to talk to my son about this difficult subject.* Sometimes it is asking for help, as if from a protector. *Please protect me from this toxic person in my life. Please keep me safe. Please help me exit this relationship.* Sometimes it is asking for a wish to be granted—a "Santa Claus prayer." *Please let my bill of health come back clean. Please help as I look for a higher-paying job. Please help me find the perfect home.*

Prayers of petition, at their core, are prayers in two parts: we ask, and then we are open to receiving. There is nothing too large—or too small—to ask for God's help with. Your newly established practice of asking—and then listening—for guidance will serve you as you work through the exercises of this week.

PRAYERS OF PETITION

Sometimes, we give thanks not for a blessing freely given to us, but for one we have requested. This brings us to the first form of prayer: the prayer of petition. Asking God for what we want, we may have an expectation that God will give it to us. This expectation is grounded in our conviction that God is generous, and in our conviction that what we ask for is reasonable—a boon in line with God's will for us. We do not ask for favors counter to God's intent for us—at least not deliberately. Instead we say, "Please grant me, if it be your will."

We pray for what we feel we need, knowing that God always meets our true needs. We are prepared, too, for our answered prayer to be met with "no." We trust the wisdom of God in granting us—or refusing us—our wishes. At least we try to trust.

"Please send me love," we may pray, desiring a romantic partner. God's response may be to send us friendships—not the form of love we had in mind, but perhaps a wiser and more fulfilling love. In cozy retrospect, we can see divine wisdom. At least we try to see.

Asking for a specific gift from God, we may experience several answers: "yes," "no," or "not now." Met with denial, we are asked to trust God's wisdom. We believe it is God's will for us to be happy, joyous, and free. Yet our requests are not always wise. They may run counter to God's good intentions. To our dismay, our destiny may be better fulfilled by God's refusal to grant our wish. And yet often, over time, God's wisdom is revealed.

It is God's intention to bless each of us. God's will for us is personal, tailored to our needs. When we pray, "This or something better," we are aligning our will with God's. The prayer for a specific good becomes subsumed by a greater good. We trust in God's wisdom—at least we try. We surrender our desire in the face of divine discretion. Our passing disappointment must be given over to faith that God knows best.

As we petition God for our wishes, we must bear in mind the firm notion that God's wishes for us may be better. Praying for a desired good, we must bear in mind always that there is not only good, but better. Praying for guidance, we might hear: "There is no error in your path. You are well and carefully led." Our faith must sometimes stretch to believe in God's benevolence. Disappointed by God's denial, we must pray further to accept God's wisdom. This is the time for a prayer of acceptance: the serenity prayer. "God, grant me the serenity to accept the things I cannot change, the courage to change the things I can, and the wisdom to know the difference." This prayer asks us to accept God's will.

Acceptance doesn't always mean happiness. We may be angry at God's refusal. Here, we are asked to trust that God can accept our anger. God is big enough to absorb all our feelings. We are asked here to be candid, to pray to God using our own words. "Dear God, I'm angry. I don't understand your refusal. Help me to accept your will." Sometimes such acceptance is hard to come by. And yet, in time, we do accept. After all, we have no choice.

"Dear God, teach me, tutor me, guide me," we pray in such circumstances. The one we love loves another. We ask for the wisdom to see that we are being spared. In time, the wisdom comes. More is revealed. The one we loved is shown to be fickle. We were spared heartbreak. God's will for us was merciful. Difficult as it is to see, God's will for us is always merciful. Faced with denial, we must remind ourselves of this fact. We are being tempered, led to something better. Our prayers of petition need always contain a dose of humility. "Dear God, give me what I ask for—or something better."

Bowing to the wisdom of God, we experience a surrender of our own will. Surrender brings with it peace. We stop fighting for our own way. We may feel sorrow that our wish is not granted, but we also feel curiosity. Just what does God have in mind for me?

I have a friend who prays daily for ease and joy. Her petition is often granted, and when it is not, she bows to the evident need for hardship. Her daily surrender to God's plan gives her equanimity. She doesn't insist on her own agenda. Instead, she gives way to the evident agenda of God.

I pray daily that God "guard and guide me, give me faith and optimism, and give me everything I need." Having thus prayed, I take what comes. I ask for "knowledge of God's will for me and the power to carry that out." I try not to fight with the day as it unfolds. Sometimes, however, I argue with God's timing. After all, I not only want what I want, I want it *now*. But then I am reminded to pray for patience. I remember that God has the long view. God's will may involve waiting as the answer to my prayer of petition is "not now." Not, perhaps, never—but definitely not now.

I am a playwright, and I sometimes must wait years for a production. I petition God, "What about my plays?" and I "hear," "Your plays will find homes." There is no mention of when or where, and so I wait, sometimes impatiently, for a venue to open up. Praying on the page, I listen for further clues. I am told my future venue will be practical, prestigious, and esteemed. A venue does open up, but it is for a theater located two hours west of Seattle by ferry. It doesn't sound practical, prestigious, or esteemed. Can it be God's will for me? The theater offers me a staged reading in February—a cold ferry ride—and a production in October. I have already had a staged reading, and the October dates conflict with a long-promised teaching engagement in Scotland. Too little and too tortured, I decide. Not God's will for me. I will wait—and hope—for another theater to open up. I will petition God for help with my plays, believing in the reality of divine intervention.

I've come to believe that our prayers are always answered, but I believe, too, that the answers are sometimes subtle. When we petition God, we are voting for our own worthiness. We are asserting that God pays attention to our prayers, and that we are worthy of our prayers being

Pray, and let God worry.
—MARTIN LUTHER

heard. Here is where the direction to pray in our own words may be most valuable. Again, I pray as "LJ," short for "Little Julie," and then I make my request. And so, a prayer may go:

LJ: Can you guide me about my plays?

I pray, and then I listen for a response. In this case, I hear, "There is a place for you in the theatrical world. Your plays will find homes." I take this response to be a promise. My prayer has been answered with hope for the future.

When we make a prayer of petition, we hope. We hope that our prayers will be answered in the affirmative. Our hope is in itself a prayer, the yearning of our heart. If we believe, as I do, that God is all-knowing, then God knows our hope—the hope that is in our heart. Responding to that hope is God's business. If a prayer is answered with "no," that is a merciful answer in our own best interests. Praying to God, the Higher Power, I am told, "Do not doubt my goodness." Faced with a "no," we may in fact doubt God's goodness. We may need to pray again, this time for greater faith. We have been taught to pray, "God, I believe, help my disbelief." This prayer directly addresses our occasional lack of faith—a normal human failing.

A friend of mine scared me recently. We were talking about prayer, and she said she doubted that God had ears for the prayers of a "puny little two-legged creature." I wanted to assure her, "Oh, but he does." Faced with her disbelief, I found myself thinking, "I believe in a listening God." And I do. Writing my prayers on the page, I ask, "Can I hear from the Higher Power?" I receive a prompt response.

"Julia, I speak to you directly." Is this my imagination? I think not. The words form without effort on my behalf.

My friend Jacob Nordby, a spiritual writer, tells me he, too, prays on the page, and he, too, receives answers to his prayers. Kindred spirits, we are agreed that praying on the page elicits a response. More people should try it, we further agree. The direct—and personal—response from God builds faith. Over time, the guidance is persuasive. God's voice is clear and direct. We are indeed led carefully and well. "There is no error in your path," we are told, and we come to believe it. The written word has a gentle authority. Reading back over our guidance, we come away feeling reassured. God is listening, we conclude—listening and responding.

In order to hear our prayers answered, we must be willing to believe. We pray, and we entertain an expectation that our voice will be heard. When our voice is responded to, we know we are in communion. We pray "Dear God," and God answers—and answers promptly. If we write to God, our written word carries weight. When we petition God, our request is heard. We come to believe in a listening God. We experience a dialogue. We talk to God, and God talks back. The divine voice is simple and direct. We hear it clearly, without strain. The ease of our communication may surprise us. Why do we imagine that prayer must be difficult?

◄ TRY THIS ►

Take pen in hand. Address God directly: "Dear God," and then broach a subject on which you feel you need guidance right now, in this very moment. "What should I do about X?" you may query. An answer will come to you, often addressing an unspoken concern. As a sober alcoholic, I have been told, "Rest assured in your sobriety. You are sane and sober." Until that response, I wasn't aware of a lingering fear of drinking, a concern that I might be crazy. And so, asking to hear about "X"—my writing—I am assured of my soundness of mind, a prerequisite to writing with confidence—a requirement that God knew well. By exchanges like this one, the wisdom of God is revealed. God, after all, is God—believed by many to be all wise, all knowing.

THE HUMILITY OF PRAYER

When we pray, we tacitly acknowledge God as creator, and us as his creations. We are humble enough to ask for help. At its root, prayer is an acknowledgment of our limitations. We defer to a power greater than ourself, asking for divine aid. Prayer is a great paradox. By humbling ourselves, we are lifted up. In the act of surrendering to a Higher Power, we are given the power necessary to lead a successful life.

When we pray, we ask for support. We acknowledge our limitations. Reaching for God, we ask for grace, and grace is given to us. We tap into a power greater than our purely human resources. God is all-powerful, and freely shares that power with us as supplicants. When we ask for strength, we are given strength, often facing down situations which used to baffle us.

I ask God to guard and guide me and my beloveds. This prayer acknowledges God's benevolence. I trust God's goodwill on our behalf. As the silver disc of a full moon rises over Santa Fe's mountains, I am reminded of God's great kindness to gift us with such beauty. Surely the God who created the moon in its many phases can be trusted to guide our course as well. The same power that steers the planets in their course can steer our lives. And so we pray, "Build with me and do with me what you would," trusting that God's will for us is benevolent. We surrender control.

Learn to hear your inner voice, be led by your heart and never stop giving back—this way you shall always walk the right path and shall never be walking alone.

—ALEKSEJ METELKO

Here is where we come up with an old idea. We often believe that God's will and our own are at opposite ends of the table. The thinking—if you can call it thinking— goes something like this: "I want to be a writer, but God wants me to be a waiter slinging food in a hash joint." We imagine that it is God's will for us to be not humble, but humiliated. Where do we get such an idea? God, after all, is our maker, and part of what is made is our heart's desires. Our yearnings may have been given us to be fulfilled, not denied. It may please God to give us our heart's desires. And so when we pray, "Build with me and do with me as you would," we may be praying to be made authentically ourselves. Take me: I write for a living. It brings me joy. And when I pray to have my writer's dreams fulfilled, it may be that I am praying precisely for God's intention for me. After all, God, not self-will, made me a writer.

A good look at God's blossoming world can convince us that we, too, are intended to blossom. Regard the tulip, the peony, the rose, the aster, the violet—each blooming happily according to its nature. So, too, each human being has gifts and characteristics that are intended to be fulfilled. We were not created to be thwarted. Rather, we were made for a full flowering. And so when we pray, "Thy will be done," we are asking for our own nature to be fulfilled. If we can still be said to be petitioning God, we are petitioning God to do as God pleases. Ironically, what pleases God may please ourselves as well.

I started writing full-time at age eighteen. Twelve years later, at thirty, I prayed, "What shall I do next?" meaning, "Give me a writing idea." Instead, I got a marching order: I was to teach.

"Oh, no!" I exclaimed. "I want to be an artist, not a teacher."

But the marching order persisted: teach. And so, reluctant but obedient, I set about teaching creative un-blocking, little realizing that in teaching unblocking, I would myself be rendered unblocked. I would conse-quently flourish as an artist. Teaching—which I didn't want to do—would lead me to greater and greater cre-ativity. God's will for me neatly fulfilled my own.

It's now forty years since I started teaching. I have come to love teaching nearly, if not quite, as much as I love writing. It is a great pleasure to me to watch the tools take hold. Traveling internationally, I teach in person, and I teach now through my books, marrying teaching and artistry, most notably through *The Artist's Way.*

"I love teaching," I recently told someone who in-quired why, after four decades, I was still teaching. And I do love teaching, often recalling ruefully my initial rejec-tion of God's direction.

I have come to believe that God is patient, well able to withstand our defiance. If God is patient, we are stub-born, most especially in matters of the heart. "Please let my love be reciprocated," we pray, when clearly our love is not. "Please, oh please," we pray, rather than surren-dering to the obvious fact of our rejection. If it is indeed God's will for us to be happy, then it is clearly God's will that we practice acceptance, that we surrender our self-will, recognizing that love can come to us from many sources—perhaps chiefly from God. If, as we are so often told, God is love, then we do well to go to God to salve our broken heart.

There is no pain too great for God to soothe it. The loss of a child, like the loss of a love, can be healed by God's grace. Acceptance comes to the willing heart. Faced with tragedy, we can seek God's silver lining. Even the death of a loved one can be met with faith if we are willing to try. I am thinking now of my friend Maria, who survived her daughter's suicide by prayer. Praying, she realized that her tortured child was now at peace.

Prayer is the cry of the heart for grace. Grace is God's gift in response to our plea. Grace moves us from defiance to acceptance. "It wasn't meant to be," we tell ourselves of the lover who spurned us. "It was her time," we say of an untimely death. As we surrender to higher wisdom, we experience a "letting go." We let go of our will and accept God's.

"Let go and let God," we are advised when we cling to a desired outcome. Loosening our grip on events, on people, places, and things, we experience relief. As we practice the fine art of surrender, we tell ourselves, "If not this, something better." Curiosity overcomes our dismay. Just what is God up to?

Waking, we may face a day fraught with difficulties. Prayer is in order. "Please give us knowledge of your will for us and the power to carry that out." This is a heartfelt request for grace, and grace dismantles the day's difficulties. It is a boon. We come to realize that God is doing for us what we could not do for ourselves.

"It was a God shot," we sometimes acknowledge when faced with what feels like divine intervention. We dare to pray for help, and then we dare to recognize that help when it comes. "Please give me words," we may ask when faced with a difficult conversation. And later we say "Thank you" because the words indeed came.

Praying daily on matters large and small, we come to believe in answered prayers. As our lives work out, we begin to see that their working out is a direct result of our asking for help. "Guide me and guard me," we pray, and then we experience our lives as guided and guarded. As we establish and experience a conscious contact with God, we are rewarded with clarity. We intuitively know how to handle difficult situations. The hunch, the instinct, the intuition gradually becomes a waking part of the mind.

Hopes, wants and wishes, all cast across the night sky with my heart in tow.

—JAY LONG

We come to rely upon it. The "still, small voice" becomes louder. We have formed a working partnership with God.

As we quit playing God and become open to God's leadership, our lives straighten out. Established on such footing, we become teachable. God is the teacher; we are God's pupils. We learn to pay heed to subtle cues to direct our path. When we are listening to God, we experience a sense of "rightness." When we are disregarding God, we experience a "funny feeling" that we are off-kilter. Over time, we depend on this guidance. We check in almost automatically with our question, "What should I do next?" By allowing God to guide us, we move through our day more smoothly. We no longer take mental cigarette breaks while we figure out our next step.

Often, when we ask God to direct our days, we find ourselves moving in unexpected directions. We will have a hunch to do such and such, only to discover our hunch is perfectly timed. "Call so and so," we may be directed, only to find that our call was welcome and again well-timed. God is the great harmonizer. God's will is earmarked by ease.

A friend of mine rises at dawn, then sits quietly praying for God's will, asking that it unfold with "ease and joy." She has sustained this practice for three decades, and her life is indeed characterized by ease. She travels widely, and her travels always go smoothly. "I'm never afraid," she tells me, drawing strength from her daily practice. "I believe God's will for me is good," she adds, "and that's what I experience."

Oh Lord, won't you buy me a Mercedes Benz?

—JANIS JOPLIN

It's my belief that her daily practice has taught her that God's will is benevolent. The ease of her life is an answered prayer. When she travels, which is often, she keeps to her routine, rising at first light and forging conscious contact. It does bring her ease and joy.

Another friend of mine also has a life that unfolds with daily grace. "I pray," he tells me, "throughout the day, but instead of saying, 'Thy will, not mine, be done,' I have amended the prayer to suit me better. I pray, 'May my will be thy will.'" His personalized prayer contains the optimistic assertion that his will and God's will may coincide. It is less forbidding than "Thy will, not mine, be done," which has a hint of antagonism—the faint suggestion that God's will and our own are somehow in opposition.

It is perhaps a remnant of our Calvinistic culture that suggests our will is typically in opposition to God's. It is both a pessimistic and Calvinistic view to hold that our base nature harbors desires which are counter to God's intention. How radical—and comforting—to posit that our desires may somehow mesh with God's.

Yet another ninety-year-old friend of mine is a fifty-seven-year practitioner of a praying path. She exclaims to me, "Prayer is so important! I pray for my children and my friends, and then I always say a prayer or two for people who aren't praying. I will pray and say, 'This is Jane's prayer. This is Richard's.' I must tell you, though, that the most terrifying words in the English language are 'Thy will be done.' I like your friend's idea of a prayer that goes, 'May my will be thy will.' In all my years, I've never heard that, and it's so much less terrifying."

"Terrifying" is an extreme but accurate word for our fear of being at odds with God. So many of us were raised with a punitive God. If we didn't believe in hellfire, we might still believe that our basic nature met with God's displeasure. "Thy will, not mine," suggests that God is good while we are not. It implies that our will is implicitly flawed, even evil. With an authoritarian God, we thus stand judged, even condemned. It goes back as far as Genesis, when Eve plucked the forbidden apple: her will, not God's. As we imagine God's will and our human will coinciding, we pray with exuberance, trusting that our impulses might meet with God's approval.

◄ **TRY THIS** ►

It is a paradox that when we pray from a position of humility, we find ourselves most empowered. We can honestly state our wishes while acknowledging that the world is not fully in our control. Being able to state what we wish, while also accept that it is not ours to decide, puts us in a place of honesty— and in honesty, there is strength.

Fill in the following sentences:

If God's gifts were limitless, I would ask . . .

If I am honest with myself, I wish God would help me with . . .

I'm afraid to ask for God's help with . . .

I doubt that God could help me with . . .

The thing I most want God's help with is . . .

A WING AND A PRAYER

Padding into my living room with a cup of coffee, I heard it: *tweet.* Settling into the love seat to do my morning pages, I heard it: *tweet.* Distinctly, clearly, disturbingly, the *tweet* issued from my fireplace. It wasn't a mechanical sound. It was a melodic sound. *Tweet, tweet, tweet.* It was a bird.

I knew it was a bird, a trapped bird, a bird that had flown down my chimney and was crying for help. Once before I'd had a trapped bird. My handyman, Anthony Rivera, had reached into the fireplace and captured it in a towel. He had ferried the frantic, frightened bird across the living room, down the hall, out the patio door to freedom.

"Pretty," he'd announced, watching as the bird flapped heavenward.

Now, I phoned Anthony one more time for help. "Please let me reach him," I prayed. He answered.

"Anthony, I have a bird in my fireplace. This time it sounds like a songbird. Can you help me?"

"I'll come on my lunch hour," Anthony responded. "I can't come until then. I'm busy, but I'll come then."

Lunch hour was three hours away and the little bird would have to wait. *Tweet*, it entreated me but I thought, "If I go near it, it will escape the chimney and flap through the house. We'll never catch it."

And so I dressed for the day, cocking my ear to hear the plaintive *tweet,* reassuring myself that the bird was alive, merely trapped and frightened. *Tweet!* Even crying out in fear, the bird was melodic. My first bird had been big, deep throated. This tweet sounded heartwarmingly small, a tiny songbird, migrated from my piñon tree to the chimney where curiosity sealed its fate. *Tweet!* Was it my imagination or was the tiny voice growing hoarse, exhausted? I crossed to the fireplace and peered inside. It was too dark to see anything and besides, the little bird was struck mute with terror seeing a large human looming near. "It's okay, little bird," I murmured.

Two and a half hours to lunch hour and I had a doctor's appointment to go to. With luck I would be back in time to meet Anthony. I left for my appointment an hour early. I would explain to the receptionist about the trapped bird and meeting Anthony. Minutes ticked past and I sat impatiently in the waiting room. No matter that I'd arrived early. The doctor was running late. At last the nurse called me, "Julia?" I was shown to a small examining room. Obedient but anxious, I did as directed. The doctor entered and brusquely set about my exam. "Hurry!" I willed her.

"You're fine," she pronounced, finally leaving me to hurry into my clothes.

Driving home, I thought of Anthony. What if he came early? I pushed the speed limit thinking of the bird still trapped, still frightened. Entering the house, I listened for the frantic *tweet*.

Silence. Had the little creature somehow navigated back up the chimney to freedom? What if it had succumbed to shock? SILENCE. I phoned Anthony to tell him the bird was gone or dead.

"I'm almost there. I want to check the flue. If it's dead, it will rot and stink."

I pictured Anthony retrieving a tiny corpse. I sat waiting for him in my living room across from the silent fireplace. Dead, I concluded. The victim of shock.

Anthony rapped at my door. He was cordial but businesslike. He went straight to the fireplace.

"I'm going to open the flue and then it will fly out," he announced. I told him I thought the bird was dead.

"We'll see," he pronounced briskly, moving aside the fireplace screen, ducking into the fireplace to open the flue.

Let your wishes be your prayers.

—LAILAH GIFTY AKITA

Whoosh! What's this? A tiny bird zoomed from the fireplace into the living room. It flapped against the largest window, frantic to escape. Quick! With a single lunge, Anthony captured the bird. He held it tenderly in his cupped hands.

"I'll get the door!" I announced, and Anthony, the bird, and I made it to the doorway. I got a quick glimpse of its tiny, red-breasted beauty, then I opened the door and Anthony took three quick steps outdoors, opened his hands, and shooshed the little bird to freedom. It darted from his hands upward to the sky.

"Good work, Anthony," I caroled.

"Pretty," he announced proudly.

"Thank you, God, for Anthony," I prayed. "And thank you for the safety of the little bird."

◄ TRY THIS ►

What could you use help with, right now, in your own home? Nothing is too small.

Fill in the following sentences:

Right now, in my own home, I'd like God's help with . . .

Right now, in my own home, I'd like God's help with . . .

Right now, in my own home, I'd like God's help with . . .

Right now, in my own home, I'd like God's help with . . .

Right now, in my own home, I'd like God's help with . . .

IF IT BE THY WILL . . .

It is a cold, clear night and a full moon rises over the mountains. The moon casts a silvery light on my courtyard. My juniper tree stands out, inky black. All in all it is a blessed night. Stars sparkle in the western sky. The moon rise is in the East. "Thank you, God," I breathe in the beauty. "Thank you."

My guidance has told me to write more on prayers of petition. What is there to say? When we petition God we are asking for something. We desire a certain object or outcome. We are asking that our desire be heard and that God, generous God, will grant our wish.

Prayers of petition count upon God's goodwill. We do well to pray with an addendum: "This, please, if it be thy will." The addendum guarantees that we are not dictating to God. We are asking a boon of God but only if it is in line with divine intent.

And so we pray, asking God for our authentic desires, standing before our creator humble and vulnerable, acknowledging that God is all-powerful, able to grant our desires. As we petition God for our wishes, we are tutored as to the worthiness of our requests. When we pray, "If it be thy will," we are given the opportunity to examine the purity of our petition. Some wishes are clearly more worthy than others. And so when we pray, "This, if it be thy will," we are given the chance for self-seeking to slip away. The desires that pass muster, selfless not selfish, are desires that meet with God's impulse to give. Remembering that God is generous, we can expect a desired outcome. We are praying, after all, that our will and God's coincide.

God is our creator and knows the wishes of our hearts. When we articulate those wishes we stand naked before God. Our humility in asking for our desires places us squarely in God's sight, surrendered. Acknowledging our hopes and needs, we acknowledge God's omnipotence. As we surrender our wishes to higher wisdom, we offer an act of worship.

A prayer of petition implies intimacy with God. Asking for our desires, we expect to be understood. We ask for what we want, counting on God's benevolence. We are, indeed, children of the creator and, childlike, we trust the creator's goodwill. Our hearts are known to God and God, fount of all wisdom, grants our heart's worthy desires. Our answered prayers teach us our maker's intention for our highest good. We learn to pray, "May my will be thy will." Passing through our days, we pause to say, "Thy will be done." That is our highest petition and we have been tutored to desire it.

The moon has risen high in the sky. It is a luminous disc announcing the power of its maker. As I write of

Why do we pray our wishes to God?
Because then our desires seem possible.

—RICHELLE E. GOODRICH

prayer of petitions, I think of the boldest form our petitions may take—in affirmative prayers.

Ours is largely a Calvinist culture, punitive and filled with self-loathing. Spiritually, we often wear a cloak of self-contempt. We lecture ourselves that our dreams and desires are egotistical. We scold ourselves for our wants. We focus on the flaws in our desires, the "ego" that they reveal. Affirmative prayer, by contrast, teaches us to believe in a benevolent and supportive world, a world friendly to our dreams and desires.

The great spiritual teacher Ernest Holmes, founder of the movement Science of Mind, believed in and practiced affirmative prayer. His prayers were positive, uplifting, and instructive. He believed in God's goodness and our own. His prayers connect adversity to opportunity, connect loss to gain, connect sorrow to wisdom. They are powerful and expansive. "My will *is* thy will," they proclaim. Clear-eyed and clear-headed, they assume the best from God and from ourselves.

In 1934, Holmes published a tiny but powerful volume, *Creative Ideas.* When it was re-published in 2004, it was my honor and privilege to write the foreword, introducing Holmes's ideas to a new and broader audience. My book, *The Artist's Way,* was grounded in Holmes's principles. He believed, as I do, that prayer was claiming our birthright.

"With divine help, all is always well," affirmative prayer declares. It invites us to cast off our shame; it's an old coat. Instead we are asked to believe that we are a fountain, a mountain in the sun. Our heart is the "velvet case where birds sing."

As Holmes writes, "I affirm that today is filled with blessings for myself and others." And further, "I am guided now into right action and successful accomplishment of all my good desires." And further still, "This I accept. This I experience." And more, "I know that the

creative law of good is infinite and has all power to accomplish. I know its whole desire for me is freedom and
joy." He concludes, "The infinite richness of one Spirit is
mine to enjoy."

Reading Holmes, one's mood rises. He claims good and
good is immediately felt. God is all-powerful, he asserts,
and all the power of God is at our disposal. There is no limit
to what we can accomplish through God. We have good
reason for optimism. He concludes his book of prayers on a
high note: "Life now sings through me in radiant ecstasy."
Using prayers, we experience the same jubilation.

◄ **TRY THIS** ►

Using affirmative prayers is a fast and powerful way
to put us in touch with both our dreams and the
divine. An affirmative statement is a positive statement of a desire as if it is already so. Create for
yourself five short affirmative prayers. For example:

1. I am an often-produced playwright whose
work is both moving and thought-provoking.

2. I have a life-long, strong and steady relationship with my niece.

3.

4.

5.

TRUSTING GUIDANCE

It takes practice to learn to trust the guidance we hear.
There are always times when our human worry will take
over, and it is in these times that we must especially try to
ask for—and listen to—a Higher Power. Our anxiety is
quelled when we allow a higher voice of wisdom to speak.

Over and over, I have learned that my human concerns can be soothed by guidance—and that my guidance turns out to be right. And yet, I still have moments where I struggle to trust the still small voice that is assuring me that things are, ultimately, okay.

The day is bleak and I am anxious. I woke early and was unable to sleep again. "How is Jeannette?" eddied in my mind. We had had a date to talk last night at 9 p.m. and she neither answered nor called. At 11 p.m., I left her a message that I was turning in and would talk to her tomorrow. That's now today and still no answer and no call. Jeannette is a doctor and she could have had an emergency call. That would explain last night, but today? Maybe she has telephone trouble, I guessed. But it seemed unlikely that both of her phones would be dead. And so, "How is Jeannette?" eddied through my consciousness. Troubled, I turned to prayer.

"Dear God, please let Jeannette be okay," I prayed. Immediately, I felt my mind start to relax. I heard, "There is no cause for alarm." I tried to believe it. Next, I prayed to my mother, who I believe looks after my friendship with Jeannette. My mother, Dorothy Shea, would have loved Jeannette's optimism and honesty. "Dear Mom," I prayed, "please look after my friend Jeannette." I heard, "Jeannette is fine. She had an emergency to cope with."

My phone shrilled. It was Jeannette calling me from a subway station in Queens. She used my mother's language: "I had an emergency to cope with." She explained that she had received an SOS from a friend suffering pneumonia. She had made an emergency late-night house call from Manhattan to Queens. They had gone straight to the emergency room. "Here comes the train. I'll call you when I get home," she said in a rush. The phone went dead.

"There's no cause for alarm," I remembered my guidance telling me. That, and "Jeannette is fine." I was dismayed that it had taken a phone call from Jeannette herself to put my mind totally at ease. I had prayed and heard answers. Why was it so hard to accept my guidance? I prayed again: "Dear God, why don't I trust you?"

I heard: "Little one, your need is for safety."

I asked: "Why can't I find safety in you?"

I heard: "Have compassion for yourself. Fear is human."

I said: "It may be human but it's hard."

I heard: "Further prayer is the answer."

And so, waiting for Jeannette to call me back, I prayed, "Dear God, please remove my fear. Help me to find safety in you."

Outside my windows, the bleak day was brightening. The mountains loomed, steep and majestic. I thought of God, their maker. The hand that created the mountains could cradle my fear. God's hand was bold, yet tender.

"There's no cause for alarm," I heard divine reassurance again. This time, I believed it.

THREE TIMES A week I work out with a trainer, Michele Warsa. Normally full of good cheer, she arrived today looking worried. "Julia, I'm freaking out," she announced. "I think my hip is going bad." She pointed to a spot on her right thigh, wincing as she touched the site.

"Two days ago, it hurt a little. Today it *hurt*." The veteran of one hip surgery, she dreaded another. "Here, let me show you a picture." She flipped through images on her iPhone, stopping at an image of her left hip. She held out the phone in a gingerly fashion, as though the image itself hurt.

"That's metal?" I asked her. The image was of a large bolt.

"It's metal. Going into my femur," she confirmed. "I was only out three weeks," she added proudly. "I'm glad I never got addicted to pain pills. They gave me so many drugs I hallucinated. I saw a cartoon character, Bart Simpson, strolling at my nurse's side. I knew I was hallucinating, but still."

Drug and alcohol free, Michele hated to "pollute" her system. Now she put her pain to one side and focused on my workout. Putting me through my paces, she favored her right side slightly. I knew better than to tell her her pain was nothing. Instead, I sympathized. *Please guard and guide Michele*, I silently prayed. Recently divorced, Michele confessed she was without insurance, another worry. She would need insurance before they could operate. Her pretty features frowned. Why must life be so hard?

At Michele's urging, I climbed onto my exercise bike. I peddled briskly for five minutes. Then I switched to my treadmill for another seven and a half. Michele put me through weight lifting and then stretches. My chronically sore back was "fixed" by her routine.

During my workout, UPS had delivered three heavy boxes of water. "Let me help you," Michele volunteered. Scissors in hand, she undid the boxes, hefting the water into the house. "It's no trouble, really," Michele announced, forgetting her hip pain as she carried in the water.

"Thanks so much for the help," I told her. Her tiny frame was much stronger than my own. She was an advertisement for her athletic skills.

"I'm strong," Michele was fond of announcing. And the ease with which she hefted the heavy water bottles proved her point.

"I pray for you daily," I told her. "Near daily. I pray that you have all good things, all blessings, and everything you need." That includes insurance, I thought.

"Thank you," Michele responded. She believed in a compassionate God that looked out for her welfare.

"Can the pain be caused by sleeping funny?" I asked her.

"No. I don't think so. I'm sleeping fine."

"Extra prayers then," I told her.

"I'll see you Tuesday at two," she announced, back to her normal, cheery self.

"'Til Tuesday." I watched her as she crossed the courtyard. Was she limping? Perhaps slightly. "Please help Michele," I sent up a prayer. I had faith that a compassionate God would.

IT SNOWED IN the night, a deep snow, and now it is snowing again. The piñon tree, already burdened, bows its branches. A few small birds seek refuge in its interior. It's midafternoon and the snow is predicted to continue past nightfall. Temperatures are plunging and the unplowed roads will be icy. Between the snow and the ice, there will be no getting out.

The little dog, daunted by the storm, curls up in a corner behind my coatrack. When the snow abates, she will venture out—but not now.

My phone shrills, breaking the hush of the day. It is my friend Ezra Hubbard, phoning me from sunny southern Florida. "I could use some snow," he tells me. "Today, down here, it's hot. I envy you your cold."

"And I envy you your palm trees," I respond.

"Yes, it's always greener," Ezra answers me, chuckling.

He is calling to report on the great success of his recent one-man art show and to tell me he has just picked up a commission check from a client.

"So I'll be able to block out time to work on the piece."

Ezra is elated. I am elated for him. Each milestone in his career is cause for celebration. Twenty years a veteran on a spiritual path, he remembers to have gratitude for each forward step. But the velocity with which his career

Never forget to make a wish, Malte. You should never give up wishing.

—RAINER MARIA RILKE

is building has caught him by surprise. He tells me he is seeking a mentor, someone who can help him to stay grounded. He fondly recalls a mentor who has passed and who always kept him grounded.

"Try to contact him," I urge. "Write 'Can I hear from _____?' and then listen—but I think you'll need a living mentor as well."

"Yes. I've boiled it down to three choices. I'll interview them, then choose."

I can hear Ezra's complicated mental debate. I cut him short as he details the pros and cons of each candidate.

"Pray for guidance," I advise him. "Don't get too heady. You're intellectual enough. You want someone who keeps it simple, who speaks to you from the heart, not the head."

"Point taken," Ezra replies. "That's a really helpful nugget."

Glad to have been helpful, I get off the phone. I believe that Ezra can trust his guidance—and that he will indeed be able to "hear" what he needs to know and do. Once again the hush of the day descends upon my house. The little dog creeps out from her hiding place. She jumps up beside me, stares out the window at the snow, falling now in big slow flakes, beautiful.

◄ **TRY THIS** ►

Take pen to page and bring to mind a time when your worry was unfounded. It is human nature to worry sometimes, and especially when we cannot find the answers we seek, our imagination can run wild while we wait for clarity to arrive. Fill in the following sentences:

I remember when I was so worried about _____.

I had an instinct that_____.

I turned out to be right about _____.

I turned out to be wrong about _____.

When everything turned out to be okay, I felt _____.

What are you currently worrying about? What does your guidance have to say about it? Fill in the following:

Right now, my biggest worry is_____.

I am afraid that _____.

What I am really afraid of is _____.

When I ask for guidance, I hear _____.

An action I can take based on my guidance is _____.

Fill in the following:

A time when my guidance was right was when . . .

A time when my guidance was right was when . . .

A time when my guidance was right was when . . .

A time when my guidance was right was when . . .

A time when my guidance was right was when . . .

WRITING AS AN ACT OF PRAYER

The day is foggy. The mountains are blotted out and a wet snow falls. The snow will continue until 7 p.m. and the driving will be tricky. I put pen to page and strive to accurately describe the messy weather. The piñon tree looms against the fog. Birds take shelter amid its branches. They flutter when the wind shifts and the wind shifts often. It is a day to stay indoors. It is a day for writing.

"What should I write about?" I ask the page. Listening, I hear, "Write about writing." And so I wait for the next thought to unfold. I write by hand and that brings me clarity. Writing by computer is faster but less accurate and so as I pray, "How should I write?" I am told, "Take pen to page." There is a direct line from my heart to my hand. As I strive to write accurately, each thought as it unfolds, I am given, thought by thought, a path. My writing comes to me as an unfurling prayer. "Please, God, let me write what you would have me write," I pray, and the praying and the writing are intertwined. "Please give me accuracy," I ask, and the words come to me as a steady flow. "Let me be led," I pray, and I am led. I ask for guidance and I receive it.

"Pray on the page," I am tutored and so I ask, "What next?" I am told in no uncertain terms that handwriting is a direct line to the divine. "Ask for help," I am mentored, and so I do ask for help on the matter at hand.

"Guide me, guard me," I pray and I am led forward carefully and well. No matter what issue arises I am given guidance. And so when I write, "What should I write?" I am told "Write about the joy of writing." And writing is a joy. The mind picks words like ripe apples: "This one looks delicious." Writing is an act of savoring, an act of prayer. Pen to page, each word we choose is divinely inspired. As we take care to write what is unfolding within us, the flow of words is a flow of grace. The Higher Power writes through us. When we humbly ask for guidance, our prose becomes surefooted. A higher hand guides our own. As we ask to serve by our writing, what we write becomes useful, more valuable than merely ego-driven.

No matter what your wishes, they are not crazy so long as they are not crazy to you!

—STEPHEN RICHARDS

Outside the window the snow is falling in fast, furious flakes. I chase its appearance with my prose. The foggy day thickens and so does my description of its antics. The piñon tree now stands stock-still, drenched. The wet snow coats its branches. "Dear God, please keep me safe, warm, and protected," I pray. I pad to my kitchen to heat a casserole. Its warmth reassures me. Let it be cold and gray out of doors. Inside, all is well. I put my pen to page and write prayers of gratitude: "Thank you, God, for my snug abode, for my view of the foggy scene, and my protection from its chill." My pen has a mind of its own. "Thank you, God, for giving me prayers," it writes. I listen and I hear, "You're very welcome."

I use the practice of asking for guidance—and then listening—to guide me through my life, in my interpersonal exchanges, in my marching orders for the day, and in my art. As a writer, I have learned that asking for the next word, the next idea, the next project, always yields a result. The Great Creator is indeed a co-creator: plays, songs, musicals, films, poetry, and forty-plus books later, how can I not believe?

CHECK IN

How many days this week did you do your Morning Pages? Seven out of seven, we hope!

Did you take an Artist Date? What was it? Did you feel an increased connection to your Higher Power during the date? Afterward?

Did you take your walks? What insights bubbled to the fore?

Did you try asking for guidance in writing, and then listening to the answer? What guidance did you receive? Did you try applying it? What surprised you?

PRAYERS
OF
GRATITUDE

The second type of prayer naturally follows the prayer of petition: the prayer of gratitude. Sometimes we pray in gratitude, thanking God for an answered prayer. Other times, we enumerate our gratitudes in order that we take stock and see them clearly for what they are. The practice of gratitude fills us with a sense of prosperity and abundance. In counting our many blessings, we are able to appreciate the gifts that surround us—in the form of people, nature, creative expression, and synchronicity. In examining what we are grateful for, we are asked to slow down and cherish what we may have taken for granted. This week, we will experiment with prayers of gratitude. An increased sense of well-being will inevitably be the result.

NATURE'S BEAUTY

As we begin to look at our world with gratitude, it is helpful to start by looking no further than the world around us. Whether we live in the city or the country, the Great Creator's hand is evident in every flower, every tree, every passing cloud. As I look to the natural world with gratitude, I am reminded of the Great Creator as exactly that. I have often remarked that the Great Creator—the Great Artist—shows no signs of stopping. There are not just a few kinds of trees, but many. The Great Artist has designed not one pink flower, but thousands. Not one coastline, but many—sandy, rocky, lush, bare.

A newcomer to the spiritual path tells me, "I find God in nature." She waits to be told this is wrong. "That is a good place to begin," I think to myself. We call God the creator, and we have all of creation as his handiwork. That full moon speaks to me of God's imagination. It rises to the East while a beribboned sunset graces the West with stripes of apricot, fuchsia, and lilac. The beauty of nature speaks of its creator. A star-spangled night invites thoughts of its maker. Awe may be a starting point for prayer.

"Thank you for beauty," I may pray, letting my heart lift up. Beauty, after all, is miraculous. A prayer about beauty is a prayer of a grateful heart. If there is one prayer that supersedes all other prayers, that prayer is "Thank you."

Outside my window, the quiet winter reminds me of the fact that no two snowflakes are alike. No two passing clouds are alike. This is artistry in action—always making more, always creating. I need look no further than the natural world for the inspiration of an energetic artist who creates every day.

The day dawns crystalline clear, perhaps making up for the stormy day just passed. The snow in my courtyard is crisp and deep. Ice trims the portal. Lily is awake and alert. She ventures out, and comes back in a moment later. It is cold.

"Lily, breakfast?" I ask, pouring a large scoop of dog food into her bowl. She is hungry and goes straight to work on her food, pausing only long enough to lap up water.

The morning sun gilds the piñon tree. Tiny birds bob branch to branch.

"Thank you, God," I breathe. "Thank you for this glorious morning." The mountain peaks are bright white. No clouds snag on their heights. The radiant light of the morning illuminates their crags. "Glory to God in the highest,"

For each new morning with its light,
For rest and shelter of the night,
For health and food, for love and friends,
For everything Thy goodness sends.

—RALPH WALDO
EMERSON

the morning declares. My heart leaps up. Creation is beautiful, sparking prayer. I turn to the Psalms. Their jubilant verses echo my mood. The mountains soar toward the heavens. It is easy to envision their creator astride in their heights.

If yesterday's storm was the devil's handiwork, today's dawn shouts, "Praise to the Lord!" My juniper tree is bedecked with lace. A bold raven lights on its uppermost branch, bobbing its ebony head in deference to the morning.

Finished with her breakfast, Lily scrambles to her favored perch atop the love seat. From there she has a good view of her sprawling dog yard, where a pair of squirrels scampers on the woodpile. Lily gives a throaty growl, but she doesn't go out in the cold. Let the squirrels freeze their bushy tails.

Alleluia, the morning sparkles, creation saluting the Creator. All prayers please God. Prayers of petition acknowledge God's power. Prayers of gratitude acknowledge God's generosity. Prayers of praise salute God's wonder. The holiday season finds prayers of all types ascending to the heavens. "Hosanna in the highest," I think as the sun climbs over the mountains.

◄ TRY THIS ►

Looking at your immediate surroundings, list ten beauties of nature for which you can express gratitude:

I'm grateful for my view of the mountains.

I'm grateful for my piñon tree's bounty.

I'm grateful for the blue skies.

I'm grateful for the deep red of the rosebush.

(cont'd)

I'm grateful for the heady scent of lilies on my table.

I'm grateful for . . .

I'm grateful for . . .

I'm grateful for . . .

I'm grateful for . . .

I'm grateful for . . .

GRATITUDE FOR OTHERS

The sky is blue. The day is warm. The roadside snow, banked against the curb, is melting. I have written, and now I am eager to get out of the house. When my friend Scottie calls, she suggests I take myself "on a little Santa Fe adventure." Bowing to her wisdom—and taking my own advice to take an Artist Date—I pilot my Subaru down the muddy dirt roads to town. My destination is a spiritual bookstore called The Ark. I am on the lookout for good greeting cards, blank, that I can send to my friends. I make a habit of writing to my beloveds. I want them to feel cherished and a handwritten card says, "Love you, miss you."

The Ark is tucked in a residential neighborhood and is reached by a maze of tiny streets. "Dead End," a sign on Romero Street declares, but before the dead end The Ark occupies an old adobe.

"I'm looking for greeting cards," I tell the lovely young clerk. "Do you have any?"

"Boxed or single?" she asks.

"Single."

"We have lots of them, a whole little room. Just watch your step."

And so I step into a small alcove where single cards are displayed, helpfully labeled "Wedding," "Anniversary," "Encouragement," "Get Well," and, finally, low and to the left, "Blank." I pluck a blank card with an image of owls. I pluck two, then three. My father loved owls and I have inherited his fancy. Next I select two cards of gardens and finally two cards of cats. I know the images will delight my friends. Leaving the card alcove, I spot a rack with a card inscribed with an Inuit proverb. It reads: "Perhaps they are not stars, but rather openings in heaven where the love of our lost ones pours through and shines down upon us to let us know that they are happy." I find the sentiment irresistible. I reach out often to my "lost ones" and they do assure me they are happy. I will send the Inuit cards to two friends who share my love for our deceased friend Jane Cecil, a sage elder who blessed all of our lives. The proverb is a tangible prayer.

Acknowledging the good that you already have in your life is the foundation for all abundance.

—ECKHART TOLLE

Stepping to the checkout counter, I hear a familiar voice, low and sonorous. It belongs to Thomas, a Native American chaplain.

"Thomas!" I exclaim.

"Julia!" he responds. "You look so pretty with your hair down."

Thomas himself looks good with his long hair plaited into braids. He tells the clerk of a special ceremony, knowing she may take the information to tell others.

Manning a large computer, the young clerk counts my cards. "You did well," she exclaims. I slide my credit card into the waiting machine. It registers the sale and the clerk neatly bags my cache of cards.

Driving home, I look forward to inscribing the cards. They are proof positive to my friends that they are thought of and prayed for. I buy my stamps by the roll lest I run out. It takes a single "forever" stamp per card, but sometimes I use two, just as insurance that my greetings make it across the miles.

As I enter my mountaintop abode, my phone rings. When a call comes in it's a welcome interruption of my habitual solitude. Take now: a call from Jacob Nordby.

"Julia, how are you doing?" he wonders.

"I'm good," I tell him, and I am good thanks to his call. Jacob's voice is a tender rumble.

"Writing?" he asks.

"Wrote," I reply, my tone a bit victorious.

"Ah, that's good," Jacob remarks. "I don't suppose you care to read it to me?"

Jacob's request is a welcome one. It does me good to share what I've written, particularly to share it with him, himself an estimable writer. And so I read Jacob my battle with God when I first got sober—"If it's a choice between sobriety and creativity, I don't know that I choose sobriety"—and he chuckles as I read.

"Ah, that's good," he tells me when I've finished. "I want to circle back and tell you how much I enjoy hearing what you've written."

"That's good of you to tell me. After I read you something I always think, 'Was that egotistical?'"

"Oh, no," Jacob exclaims. "Your writing gives people permission to feel what they feel. Take this piece. All of us fight with God."

Jacob chuckles again. In the time that we've been friends I've come to treasure his laughter. Just now, ruefully, he elaborates on his day's weather: rain, sleet, snow, sun. The full catastrophe. Ample grounds to fight with God. No wonder he laughed at my recital of arguing with God.

Jacob and I end our call telling each other our plans for the evening in snowy Boise and clear Santa Fe. I set myself back to writing and manage a full page before the phone rings again: Emma Lively in frigid New York, phoning in.

"Julie, how are you?" she wants to know.

"Good," I tell her. "Writing."

"I shouldn't disturb you."

"It's okay. I'm at a pausing place. How are you?"

Emma fills me in on the details of the day's rehearsal of her musical, *Bliss*. She fills me in on the progress: she and her co-creator Tyler are writing a new song, and working on a comedic monologue for their powerhouse star, Mario Cantone. Sets are being built. Music is being rehearsed. They are busy but steady. I'm glad for the update. Emma and I talk daily. I like to be current on her doings.

"We're about to buy the stage manager a birthday present," she concludes her tale of the day's adventures. "We're at the M&M store. His job is so intense, we think he needs a silly treat." As they settle upon a merry rainbow-hued gift, I wish Emma a festive evening and hang up the phone.

I have calls in to Domenica, my daughter, and to my good friend Gerard. Living in Santa Fe, far from them in Chicago and New York, I value our phone calls. When I come home after having been out, I hurry to check my messages. Domenica's goes, "Hi, Mommy. I love you." Gerard says he's in for the night and would welcome a call. I send cards to my far-flung friends regularly, but the telephone remains our principal means of communication. I place a call to Gerard and one to Domenica, blessing AT&T.

I WAS SEATED at my dining room table eating a late dinner when I saw it: a tiny gray flash. It dashed behind a bookshelf and Lily gave chase, woofing with worry. She had been woofing for two days, and now her behavior made sense. Nose to the floor, sniffing, she was hunting. A mouse was in her domain.

Where there was one mouse, there were more. Lily had woofed by the piano, woofed by the couch, woofed by the kitchen cabinet. It suddenly seemed to me there were mice everywhere. Lily felt the same, woofing with anxiety, rushing hither and yon. "God help me," I prayed. I was jittery. I needed help, but it was late, too late to do anything that night. Panicked, I dialed the number for Anthony, my handyman. He was coming in the morning to repair my courtyard gate that was gaping open. He had saved the trapped bird. Could he also help with mice?

Anthony answered his phone, although he was out to dinner with his wife, Carmella. "Anthony," I blurted. "I have mice!" I told him about the gray flash and Lily's agitated hunting. He listened patiently and waited for my own agitation to die down. Then he spoke.

"I'll bring supplies to trap them when I come to fix the gate," he said calmly. "We'll be able to get rid of them."

And so the next morning Anthony arrived, armed with traps and a jar of peanut butter. "Mice love peanut butter," he explained. "But so does Lily. I'll put the traps where she cannot get at them—behind the piano, behind the bookshelf, behind the kitchen cabinet, and behind the water heater."

Anthony had a plan. He would set the bait and then come back tomorrow to check on his traps. I was still spooked, although Anthony was both confident and competent. I fled the house, leaving him to his work. I drove down the mountain to Love Yourself Cafe where a bowl of oatmeal awaited my arrival. I was still spooked but ravenous. I gobbled up the oatmeal and planned to drive back up the mountain to home. I got to my feet and felt suddenly dizzy. My vision seemed blurry although I was wearing my glasses—the better to spot a gray flash. Squinting to see clearly, I drove with care. What was wrong? I felt hot and then cold. "Let me make it home," I prayed.

Opening the door to my house, I found Anthony still at work. He was just blockading a final trap to thwart Lily's hunting. I wobbled on my feet, dizzy again.

"Anthony, I'm dizzy," I blurted out.

"Sit down," Anthony commanded. "Drink some water. Take a few deep breaths and drink more. You're probably dehydrated."

Anthony handed me a bottle of water. I gulped it down. I drew several deep breaths, then drank some more. Instantly, I felt myself steadying. I got to my feet. The dizziness was gone.

"There. You look better," Anthony announced. "You just needed water."

"What do I owe you?" I asked gratefully. "For the gate and the mice."

"Nothing. The gate is a present. Keep drinking water and I'll see you tomorrow."

"You're a godsend, Anthony," I told him. And I reflected that he was literally "God sent." Panicked over the mice, I'd prayed, "God help me." And God—and Anthony—had.

We must find time to stop and thank the people who make a difference in our lives.

—JOHN F. KENNEDY

◄ TRY THIS ►

List five people you are grateful for and why. They may be from your present or your past.

I am grateful for _____

because _____.

I am grateful for _____

because _____.

I am grateful for _____

because _____.

I am grateful for _____

because _____.

I am grateful for _____

because _____.

DEAR GOD, PLEASE HELP MY MOOD

As my prayer life deepened after I got sober, I found myself "reporting in" to God with increasing candor. "I'm grumpy," I prayed, believing God to be receptive to all my moods. "I'm happy to be writing," I might confess, certain that God would be pleased with my productivity, as I was myself. "Help me to straighten up the house," I asked this afternoon, and I experienced an answered prayer as I was willing to tidy up.

With the house neatened up, I was able to focus one more time on the beauty of my surroundings. A full moon was rising over the mountains. Its silvery light washed my courtyard, illuminating my garden, where snowy lilies stood sentinel. This habit of "reporting in" to God is a habit I maintain, forty-two years later.

Praying for a change of mood strikes me as petty but useful. Moods, after all, float in like clouds, and I am accustomed to feeling powerless under their weight. Asking for divine help makes me feel less a victim. If moods are mysterious to me, they are evidently less mysterious to God. With God's help, they can be changed, not simply endured. With God's help, I am no longer powerless. My dark mood can brighten. No longer oppressed, I can find myself grateful. The change of mood, like a change of scenery, tutors me in joy.

God knows my moods and is responsive to my need to alter them. God's compassion is evident as my depression lifts. Mercy is an apparent trait of the creator. My plea for help does not go unanswered.

"Please help my mood" is a legitimate prayer, not a petty one. Moods, after all, are powerful, and relief from a dark mood is a request the creator honors. A dark mood runs counter to God's intent for us. The relief of such a mood is a grace. Trusting that God is merciful and compassionate, I again make my request for a lighter heart.

Gratitude bestows reverence . . . changing forever how we experience life and the world.

—JOHN MILTON

I ask for relief, if not actual joy. I ask that my darkness lighten, that my grumpiness go by the boards. If not instantly, soon enough I feel a shift. From pessimism, I move to optimism—from a thankless heart to a grateful one. Instead of dwelling on the negatives, I find myself counting the positives. Sometimes mentally, sometimes on paper, I make a gratitude list, and there is so much to be grateful for—my health, my home, my work, my friends, the beauty that surrounds me if I dare to look.

Today, I woke up grumpy. My mood was sour. I blamed it on lack of sleep. I woke up in the small hours. I tossed and turned for hours, unable to go back to sleep. I was cranky, fatigued as I moved through my day. I have learned to pray at such times. "Dear God, please help my mood." I had the thought to call my friend Jeannette, who advised me to constantly focus on the positives. This practice not only lightens dark moods, it actively prevents them.

"Dark days happen," Jeannette said. "Moods pass. They are time-limited. Try not to beat yourself up for your dark mood. That will only make it darker still. Try to count the positives you accomplished despite your mood."

"Well," I tell Jeannette, "I did Morning Pages. I wrote. I exercised. I ate healthfully. I walked."

Ticking off the day's accomplishments, I felt the corner of my mood lifting. The dark cloud of depression was shifting. From self-loathing and judgment, I was moving to self-respect and appreciation. Despite my mood I had managed the building blocks of a positive day.

"Focus on the positive," Jeannette counseled. "Look at all you did accomplish despite your mood."

Jeannette rang off. I settled on my love seat and thought about her advice. I went back over my dark day. It looked less gloomy to me now as I consciously counted the positives. There were many positives I'd forgotten or ignored. I talked to my daughter who was doing well. I talked to Emma, also doing well. And what about my check-in

Joy is the simplest form of gratitude.

—KARL BARTH

with Jacob? And with Laura? I had a whole bouquet of friends who all wished me well. Thinking back over our conversations, I felt my mood palpably brightening.

"What can you do that brings you joy?" my friend Scottie recently asked me. She had, perhaps, felt my dark day coming on. Taking the advice for "a little Santa Fe adventure," I had taken myself to The Ark. Counting my positives, I added two more: breakfast oatmeal at Love Yourself Cafe and five cards written, stamped, and mailed.

"My God," I caught myself thinking. "You were productive."

I felt my self-esteem rising a notch. Changing into pajamas, I caught myself thinking, "These are nice." They were a gift from Emma. My dark day was ending on a positive note. "Thank you, God," I breathed.

A heart that is centered on joy and abundance tends to be a light heart, not a dark one. Depressive moods can not only be shifted with divine help, they can actively be prevented. The prayer, "Dear God, please help my mood," can be answered not only with a shift in mood but also by a shift in consciousness. Tutored by the Great Creator, we learn practices of joy. Counting our positives, making a habit of gratitude, we teach ourselves to be as intended, "happy, joyous, and free."

Writing this small essay, focusing on a shift in attitude, I find myself free of darkness. Even my physical fatigue is alleviated. My prayer to be helped with my mood is now an answered prayer. And so I pray again, "Thank you, God, for your help with my mood." The prayer of thanks shifts my mood even a notch higher. "Thanks again, God," I pray.

IT'S A GRAY day. The mountains are whited out. It has been snowing since dawn, tiny bitter flakes, wet but sticky. The piñon tree has collected its burden of snow. One more time, tiny birds take refuge in its inner reaches. They squabble as they vie for the best perch. Tussling with one another, they jar loose a handful of wet snow. It falls from the upper to lower branches. There it sticks. So far, we have accumulated four to five inches. The roads, unplowed, are treacherous. Icy. I call to cancel two interviews. "Good for you, stay in," one person tells me, adding, "I drove out with a four-wheel drive and it was terrible. There's more snow due at six. If you get lonely tonight, call me. I think I, too, will be staying in."

I have a phone call next from my trainer, Michele. "The roads are terrible," she exclaims. "I nearly had two accidents. I'll see you in a couple of days."

One more time, my phone rings. This time, it is my daughter, Domenica. "I'm having a blue day," she says by way of greeting.

"I had a blue day Saturday," I tell her.

"What did you do to get over it?" she asks.

"I talked to Jeannette. I can read you what she said."

"Okay." Domenica, like me, sounds dubious about the possibility of her mood ever improving.

I read her Jeannette's guidance: "Focus on the positive; count the positives accomplished despite the mood. Moods are time-limited. They pass."

As she listens, I can sense Domenica's bad mood shifting. Like me, she has a long list of positives. Ticking them off to me, I hear her thought: "I've been productive. Wow." We get off the phone, each feeling better for having connected. We are each grappling with Jeannette's insight that moods are natural, time-limited, and transient. I think to myself, cynically, being snowbound brings with it an automatic dark mood: claustrophobia. I tell myself the snow will stop. The sky will clear. The roads will become less treacherous. I tell myself that my dark day served a purpose, helping my daughter. I stare out the window at the piñon tree.

It's now 1 p.m. The snow has slowed to the barest of flurries, although more snow is promised for later. "What can I do that brings me joy?" I ask myself Scottie's question. "I can write more cards," I answer myself.

I count out my cards. I have five left. I will send them to Julie, Jennifer, Jacob, Domenica, and Gerard. Writing them out, I feel a keen sense of connection. I'm not alone. I have friends.

A light breeze now stirs the piñon tree. The little birds huddle close together at its trunk. I watch the piñon tree for cues about the weather. When its branches are bare of snow, the roads will be passable. Not yet!

I phone Light Vessel Spa, the enterprise owned by Denice Sherwin, one of my canceled interviews. I get a recorded message, no Denice. The message runs, "We are closed due to icy roads." And so with one more directive to stay in, I try to accept that, staying in, I am better safe than sorry.

The phone jingles. It is my daughter checking back in. After a barn day with her pony, she is grounded and happy. "I talked to a two-decades-plus girlfriend," she reports. "She was having a blue day much like mine. Sometimes it helps to know you are not alone." She rang off.

Two bold birds chase each other through the piñon tree's branches. It occurs to me that they are playing—happy, like my daughter, that they are not alone.

◄   **TRY THIS**   ►

A simple list of tiny wins can take us from depression to hope. I recommend using this tool anytime you have a sense of hopelessness or frustration. Look back on a time when you felt stifled—it may have been today, or a day in the past, and fill in the following:

Even though I felt _____, I still accomplished _____.

Even though I felt _____, I still accomplished _____.

Even though I felt _____, I still accomplished _____.

Even though I felt _____, I still accomplished _____.

Even though I felt _____, I still accomplished _____.

Now, read over your list. Do you notice an innate driving force of forward motion and self-preservation? Allow yourself to feel gratitude for your own resiliency. Do you sense a Higher Power's hand in this strength?

THE PATH TO GRACE

We speak of finding a path to grace while forgetting that sometimes the "path" can be quite literal. Walking brings us, step by step, closer to God and to clarity. When my friend Emma lost her beloved eighteen-year-old Westie, Charlotte, she walked—sometimes more than ten miles a day—to grieve.

"It was all I could think of to do," Emma relayed to me. And it may well have been the only thing to do. I have experienced the spiritual healing brought on by walking, and I have watched student after student experience the same. I have come to believe that no matter the question, walking can provide answers. *Solvitur ambulando*—"It is solved by walking."

GEORGE BAMFORD, WRITER and actor, sat astride in a chair on his oceanside patio. At seventy-five, a still striking man, he was dressed in casual Florida gear: an orange T-shirt and blue jeans, shoes with no socks. A relaxed and genial man, he talked easily and comfortably about prayer, for thirty years a daily practice. His prayer life began abruptly at age forty-five.

"I heard a voice—a convincing voice—say to me, 'You will pray for half an hour.' I looked around. There was no one there."

The ghostly voice sounded so firm George decided to "check it out." He stopped in a chapel where he read from a tiny book of daily reflections. The day's entry took five minutes, so he read back five entries and ahead five entries. "That was it."

Modestly, his prayer life was launched. "I did it every day from then on. I didn't question it. When my wife got cancer, I increased my time to an hour. I wrote out my personal prayer, thanking God and all that. After the prayer, I would sit, quiet for a time. Just to see what I was thinking about: money or dialogue for a new play. I didn't censor my prayer and meditation. Some people might try to empty their mind but I don't. I'd say seventy-five percent of what I think about is gratitude for all that has been given me. I'm a lucky man."

George stretched, pausing to appreciate his view of the intercostal waterway and the ocean farther on. He admired "boats and more boats, all sorts of boats." Then he turned back to the topic at hand.

"I walk four miles a day," he continued. "I began my walks at age fifty. When I start my power walks I use a mantra. I say to myself, 'I am a very good person and I deserve God's good.' I counted it once. I say the mantra eight hundred fifteen times. My father raised me to hate myself. I try to brainwash myself the other way. This practice has changed my life—definitely."

George paused again, counting out the changes wrought by prayer and affirmation. He has gone from self-hating

Let gratitude be the pillow upon which you kneel to say your nightly prayer.

—MAYA ANGELOU

to self-loving. The shift has brought him joy, relief, and productivity. His is midway across a new play, self-worth holding steady. "Writing fills my heart," he explained, and writing is another of the fruits he credits to prayer.

"I can always find a place to pray," George remarked contemplatively. "In Palm Beach it is out of doors. In New York it is in churches or on a bench on Fifth Avenue. In Indianapolis there was a place called The Lady of Fatima Retreat. When Barbara, my wife, was in chemo, I went there daily. Mary, the woman on the desk, always found me a place to pray. Then one day a woman came to the chapel. She said to me, 'Are you the man who prays?' I said, 'Yes. Every day.' She said, 'Here, take this,' and she handed me a rosary made of gimp. I still have it hanging on a lamp."

Holding the memory close to his heart, George went on to talk of a central fact concerning prayer. "I believe that prayer promotes change. I've been in therapy many years and I can tell you therapy doesn't remove shortcomings. It may give you knowledge and awareness, but the imperfections remain. I myself cannot remove them. Only a power greater than myself can bring relief."

George went on to describe how change comes to him. "I get guidance. Sometimes a voice, mostly some kind of epiphany, a realization, that something that signifies a higher intelligence, a Higher Power, is at work."

George leaned back in his chair, then leaned forward to relate a recent epiphany. "Last night there was a big orange moon. I looked at it and thought, 'What holds it up?' There's a natural power, some spiritual connection, and I'm part of that. Just as the palm trees here are a part of a natural process. In the natural world, there is a higher plan—and that includes me."

Resting his arms across his chest, George concluded his thoughts. "I'm seventy-five years old. There's something I'm supposed to do at my own speed. There's something

I'd like to offer humanity. Not to change the world, just to help it. My heart is in my writing. That's a real love for me. I just want to give something."

By removing his imperfections, prayer tutors him what to give. As he takes his daily walks, I have no doubt that he will be guided to his part in the "higher plan."

ONCE AGAIN THE setting sun gilds the mountain peaks. It is the end of a blue day and the western sky is multicolored, striped with fuchsia, purple, and gold. It is time to put pen to page, rounding up the day's events. A phone call from my daughter has left me unsettled. She told me that she censors her conversations with me. Valuing candor, I am disconcerted. Just what is she leaving out? I have prided myself on our relationship, believing that we could talk of anything and everything. Now it appears that we cannot or have not. She explains that she is "protecting" me from "harsh feelings." She doesn't want to "create a triangle" of me, her, and my ex, her father. She is right that news of her father can cause me harsh feelings. After all, there are reasons we are divorced.

Rather than push my daughter into disclosures, I accept her boundaries. She is certainly old enough to make her own value judgments. As for me, I am old enough to respect them. I lace up my shoes and turn to walking prayer to calm my unruly feelings.

"Dear God," I pray as I climb the uphill dirt road near my house, "please give my child wisdom and please give me acceptance." I think of the serenity prayer: "God, grant me the serenity to accept the things I cannot change, courage to change the things I can, and wisdom to know the difference." I cannot change my daughter's reticence. I can change my own attitude toward it and I am wise enough, counseled by the Higher Power, to know the difference.

My marriage to her father ended abruptly when my daughter was eleven months old. I raised her as a single mother, sharing information with her father, but not responsibility. Over the years we sometimes differed on our "takes" regarding parenthood, but overall, we were more frequently in accord than not. What could he be doing now that she was grown, that caused her such concern? I knew that attempts on my part to find out would only cause my daughter woe. She had her reasons for withholding information.

"Dear God," I pray as I continue on, footfall after footfall. "Please give me discernment. Please help me to mind my side of the street."

I replayed my conversation with my daughter. Had I revealed to her the depth of my upset? I thought not. Instead, I had an experience of grace, an unwarranted influx of God's wisdom, tutoring me in how to behave. Yes, it was grace that made me hold my tongue, made me forgo prying, made me respect my daughter's wishes.

"Thank you for giving me grace," I now prayed as I returned to my gate and entered my courtyard. "Thank you for wisdom and discernment."

Night settles, a dark mantle over the mountains. In the southern sky a bright star sparkles. "Give me wisdom and discernment," I pray again. Surely the Great Creator, maker of the star-spangled night, has power enough to heed my request. "Thank you," I breathe.

The grateful heart is soft, gentle, compassionate. We relate to our fellows with grace. The harsh edges of resentment melt away. We become a worker among workers, a friend amid friends. The Bible adjures us to "love thy neighbor as thyself," and this charity becomes possible as we practice gratitude. Seeing the best in our lives, we see the best in the lives of others. We extend to our fellows the benefit of the doubt. Comforted by our blessings, we bless our fellows. Grateful for our many gifts, we practice generosity, sharing our gifts. The grateful heart overflows with kindness. We are not stingy. Instead, we are benevolent, blessing all from our sense of abundance.

"Thank you, God," we pray, counting our blessings. From small to large, our blessings are gifts bestowed on us by a generous God. Our grateful hearts are the gifts we bestow back to God. We appreciate God's abundance. Our appreciation moves us to pray. And so, "thank you," we say. "Thank you."

◄ TRY THIS ►

As we seek to go through the world with grace, we turn once again to our guidance. Choose a subject that is painful and close to your heart. Lace up your shoes and take yourself on a walk. Go out with a question—perhaps, "Dear God, how should I deal with X?" Listen for an answer as you walk. Upon your return, note your insights. Do you feel the sense of a higher hand? Do you see a bigger picture? Do you sense what might be called grace?

FINDING GRATITUDE IN PAIN

As I listened to my friends speak about prayer, I noted that it is often in times of pain that the gifts of the world are also illuminated. When we can find no answers for our human suffering, it is natural to reach to a Higher Power. We search for comfort when it seems no comfort is available, for understanding when it seems there are no answers. We can actively ask God for help during these times, and we often see, sometimes in the moment, sometimes in hindsight, that we were indeed given strength and insight in our darkest hour.

Dr. Jeannette Aycock settled in at her dining room table, elbows propped. She wore a fisherman's sweater and gray slacks—weekend apparel, less formal than her working gear: shirts or dresses for when she sees patients. "A mark of respect for the hard work they are about to do," she explained. Warm-voiced and gracious, she launched into her experience of prayer.

"I was brought up Southern Baptist," she began her tale. "Prayer was always a part of my life and of my parents' life. Early on I was taught about an authoritarian God—the ten commandments, teaching children the rules. When I grew older, the emphasis was on the New Testament, on love in your heart, on grace through the Holy Spirit and Jesus Christ."

Jeannette paused to collect her thoughts, then continued. "You could follow the rules and miss the point: compassion toward others. We need more than rules. Jesus Christ and the New Testament taught forgiveness.

"Growing up in the Black church gospel tradition, there were lots of prayers. Prayer was a custom-made event, depending upon the person."

Again, Jeannette paused, then she explained, "The first step in prayer is asking for things. Seeing God as able to grant wishes. 'Give us this day our daily bread.' Mostly, 'give.' Then we move on to older prayers thanking God for what he has given. Then on to praise. 'Wow! What a great God,' raising God to greatness in a global, and universal sense. So prayer is an evolution."

Jeannette's thoughts turned to her personal journey. "For myself I had a turning point," she said. "When my husband died, I had a crisis of faith, asking, 'Why me?' 'Poor me.' Then I began to focus on how lucky I was to have had him for as long as I did. It could have been much worse. I could not have had him at all and been alone.

So much has been given to me I have not time to ponder over that which has been denied.

—HELEN KELLER

"As time passed, my prayers became more intimate. Now I talk to God in a very conversational tone—not as an authoritarian connection."

Her prayer life expanded. Her definition of prayer also expanded. "I see daily actions as prayer. Breathing is a real connection. I inhale, taking in the gift of God. I exhale my plan for the day. I have a daily practice: I get up and say a prayer of thanks for another day. I read from *Guidepost*—a magazine Norman Vincent Peale founded that tends to be positive, including scripture for the day, then action for the day. I say a brief prayer for the needs of others. I find something uplifting and focus on that.

"I tend to be positive," Jeannette continues after a beat. "I belong to Marble Collegiate Church, the 'church of positivity.' I look at the world from a positive angle. I find this very helpful no matter how dark things may appear. When I lost my husband, he was only sixty. It was a heart attack. I focused on how lucky I was to have had him."

Pushing up the sleeves of her sweater, Jeannette spoke warmly, tenderly, of her deceased mate. Then she turned back to prayer, the topic at hand.

"Prayer helps others and helps me," she declared. "It gets me outside of myself and lets me see another perspective. Guidance comes to me from a Higher Power," she went on. "I believe in a living force, a positive parent who wants the best for me and his creation. This force is forgiving and patient. God is patient with me. A great force that is benevolent and long suffering—a comforting spirit as well."

Leaning closer over the table, she spoke quietly and firmly. "Prayer doesn't have to be formal. There are minute prayers, one word: 'Help!' 'Now!' God knows what I need. Sometimes it's beyond words. I may think I should be praying 'Lord, help!'—but God knows."

Jeannette has worked as a psychiatrist for forty years. Sometimes, she says, her positivity can be annoying to patients mired in the negative. Yet she persists, praying, although she doesn't talk about spirituality to her patients. She believes, as Carl Jung believed, that "bidden or unbidden, God is here."

BEAUTICIAN FRAN GALLEGOS sits cross-legged on a comfortable chair. Her salon is cozy, with warm wood tones and taupe walls, a festive Christmas wreath hung above a window. Clad in a mint-green sweater, brown leggings, and boots, sporting an antique turquoise pendant, she wore her luxurious mane pulled back, the better to see while she works. Her fringe of bangs brushed her arched eyebrows. Her huge brown eyes filled with warmth as she talked of her prayer life—"a constant communion," she says.

"I was raised Catholic," she begins. "Twelve years of Catholic education. I thought I wanted to be a nun. We would put towels on our heads and give each other communion. I remember when I was young, Father Sierra came to the house. I told him I wanted to be a nun and he said, 'Francis, you would never last.' He was right.

"The nuns told me as a child, the Aryan race are God's chosen people—beautiful, smart, and successful. I thought, if they're God's chosen people, what am I? I had to struggle to love myself despite that." Fran frowned at the memory. She is a Hispanic beauty. She is dark-complected and -haired, anything but Aryan. She continued softly, "We had a dominant God. Not touchable. You tried to live life so as not to go to hell. Now I try to live, not to gain heaven or avoid hell, but to find what purpose the Higher Power has me to do."

Every day Fran seeks God's will for her. As she

We can complain because rose bushes have thorns, or rejoice because thorns have roses.

—ALPHONSE KARR

explained, "I journal every morning starting with prayers of gratitude. 'Thank you, God, for my snug house, my affordable mortgage. Thank you, God, that nothing hurts, that I have no sciatica. Thank you that my son—though using narcotics—is still alive. Thank you for my mother's happiness at ninety-four.'"

From her journal, Fran moves on to daily prayers. As she related them, they were an ongoing dialogue with God. "God and I are in constant communication. God is something greater than myself. I ask God to fill my emptiness with his spirit, to take away my sadness and my fear."

Shifting her legs to underneath her, Fran knelt as she continued. "I say thank you for my dog, for my abundance. I try to do one good deed a day and not get caught doing it. From God I get a sense of unconditional love. I pray for grace and trust to be able to have faith that God will take care of my needs. That it is all for the best. I try to surrender everything to God. That is my goal.

"I have a mantra," Fran went on. "Bless them and change me." She smiled ruefully. "The one thing I regret is not providing my children with a foundation that there is a God that they can go to when there's no place else to go."

Fran's large eyes filled with tears. She spoke sadly. "I didn't create a spiritual foundation. I didn't know how to or I was too busy just surviving, struggling—I was too caught up in my own stuff to recognize what was important. I see my failure to teach as an amends I want to make. I pray to be shown how."

Fran smiled again, sadly. "I write every day," she concluded. "When I want my children to open their eyes and do this or that, I pray, 'Bless them, change me,' and I leave it to God." Fran's luminous face looked surrendered. Talking of her spiritual path, she found herself at peace.

◄ TRY THIS ►

It has been said that in our darkest hour, we are the closest to the light. Bring to mind a moment when you were in a time of profound loss. Fill in the following sentences:

My biggest loss was . . .

I felt like . . .

My grief was so deep that . . .

One thing that helped me was . . .

A moment I felt the hand of a Higher Power in my darkest hour was . . .

Ultimately, I am grateful that . . .

Now, remember a moment when you were treated unfairly. It might have been an unkind word from a stranger, an encounter with the inequity of the world—choose one moment, large or small. Fill in the following sentences:

I knew the world was unfair when . . .

It made me feel . . .

I felt powerless because . . .

A lesson I learned from this was . . .

One thing I can do to claim my power is . . .

Ultimately, I am grateful that . . .

BELIEVING IN THE
GOODNESS OF THE UNIVERSE

At five o'clock on Christmas Eve, the flurries started. The forecast was snow all night. I would wake to a winter wonderland, a white Christmas. My house is quiet, but a snowfall hushes it further still. When I woke Christmas morning, the trees were laden with snow. My piñon tree dipped its branches with lace. Many tiny birds took refuge in its boughs. A billowing fog obscured the mountains. The little birds flitted branch to branch while ravens, larger and more fierce, swooped higher overhead.

"Merry Christmas, Lily," I told my little dog. She ventured outside, racing in circles in the snow, gleeful and antic. Back indoors, her antics continued. She raced room to room, zooming underfoot.

"Settle down, girl," I cajoled her to no avail. She was manic and ecstatic. The snowfall was an adventure for her. "Come on," she yipped, "this is fun. Don't just sit there!"

When I didn't budge from the love seat, she leapt to my lap, a chilly, wet bundle of good cheer.

"Breakfast, Lily," I coaxed, edging her off my lap. "Come on, girl, treats," I entreated her.

"Treats" was in her vocabulary and so she trotted out to the kitchen. I followed her, stopping to scoop up a handful of tiny, liver-flavored crackers. One at a time I tossed them across the floor and laughed as Lily went scooting after them. No matter where they landed, she pounced, gobbling up the treat, eager for more.

"No more, girl. Breakfast," I told her, scooping a cup of dog food into her bowl. The dog food is an expensive staple, gentle on her delicate stomach, purchased bimonthly from her veterinarian. Lily likes its flavor and eats it willingly. The tiny pellets make a satisfying crunch.

"Please, God, keep Lily healthy," I pray daily. "Guard me and guide me in her care." Her delicate digestion notwithstanding, Lily is a healthy dog. She goes to the vet for yearly checkups and he pronounces her "Healthy. Fine."

Breakfast finished, Lily joins me on the love seat. It affords a good view of the piñon tree with its festive aviary. The tiny birds capture Lily's attention. Unlike the ravens, which are threatening, the tiny birds spark merriment. Lily watches them, entranced. Lily is a hunter and her prey is enticingly close. Each tiny bird would make a fluffy Christmas mouthful.

CLAD IN A Christmas sweater and leggings, silken-haired blonde Laura Leddy relaxed in her recliner facing her Christmas tree. The tree gave her a childlike delight and she began her comments on prayer with her childhood.

"I grew up praying," she started off. "Prayer is associated with my earliest memories. We had a constant ritual that was very sweet. We would kneel at bedside and say two prayers: 'Now I lay me down to sleep,' and 'Angel of God, my guardian dear.' Then we would say prayers for the family elders and beloved people. Either my mom or my dad would pray with us. They were both very active in the church—Roman Catholic. My father was an usher. My mother belonged to the Legion of Mary. She would say the rosary with neighborhood women. Then we would do good works, visiting an old people's home or the Angel Guardian Orphanage."

Laura paused, enjoying the tiny twinkling lights, then she continued. "My upbringing was very religion-centered. On our school papers, we would print 'JMJ' for 'Jesus, Mary, and Joseph.' We wore scapulars. When I was little, we said asking prayers for people we knew—the man across the street who needed healing. Special requests for special people. I grew up praying."

Laura folded her hands, making a tiny steeple. She went on. "I had a turning point in my twenties. I didn't always go to mass. I replaced that with my own communion. Where I would have been going to church, I began praying on my own. At the time, my then-husband groused about my going to mass and so I stayed home. By then the church prayers had lost their meaning for me. I wanted my prayers to be more vibrant, more aligned to what was actually happening in my life. So I began a practice of personal prayer, not formal prayers by rote."

Laura stretched, gathering her thoughts to continue. "I began writing my prayers. I would write them for six months or a year, then stop. I don't know why. Now I write my prayers occasionally. If I put it to paper it's more specific. I'll sometimes notice, 'Oh, there's an answered prayer.' If someone asks me to pray for them, I frequently put it to paper to remember exactly what they've asked me for."

Laura curled her long legs beneath her. Comfortable, she spoke on. "I do pray daily, throughout the day and at night before I go to sleep. I say a lot of prayers of gratitude, being mindful of lots of blessings, big or small. I say, 'Thank you for a beautiful day.' For enough food, all my creature comforts, answered prayers, things that make life beautiful. Nature. Music. Reading. Technology. We live in an amazing time."

If the only prayer you said was thank you, that would be enough.

—MEISTER ECKHART

Stretching again, she spoke onward. "I also pray for specific things. People with health issues, who lost a loved one, who are in a difficult relationship. People who need a boost, some TLC."

Leaning forward toward her Christmas tree, Laura summed up her position. "Prayer has been a very important part of my life, always. I might not be part of an organized religion, but spirituality is a huge part of me."

THE NEXT MORNING, the storm has lifted and a blue sky arches overhead as I prepare to head downtown to meet Peleg Top—"lovely" to his friends—for a conversation on prayer at Santa Fe's Love Yourself Cafe. Icicles shimmer from the portal and deep snow billows in drifts across the courtyard. The garden gate hangs heavy on its hinges. The garden wall wears a crested wave of silvery snow. All is beauty, the quiet aftermath of yesterday's storm. A slight breeze stirs the piñon tree, sending its burden of snow sifting gently downward. By noon, its branches will be bare.

Christmas has passed but the snowy season lingers on. A leftover wreath still graces my doorway, festooned with pinecones and holly berries. When the weather warms, I will dismantle the wreath, but for now the sight of it brings me good cheer.

In Santa Fe, the season is marked by tiny colorful lights, ropes of those, and matching rows of luminaries, tiny brown bags filled with sand and candles. The central plaza is hung with many glittering lights. Their colorful display will remain in place until the Epiphany. The Basilica of St. Francis Assisi is decked out in silvery wreathes. The humbler chapel wears green and red lights, the colors of the season. On Agua Fria, a major thoroughfare, a spectacular house is lit from stem to stern with Christmas tableaus. At the rooftop, a star of David sends out shimmering strands, rivaling Agua Fria. I pass this house often, marveling at the showy beauty of its display.

I tuck myself into a corner table and retrieve my notebook. Dressed in shades of gray that match his nearly barbered beard, Peleg settles in across from me over a bowl of oatmeal and begins to speak in earnest about prayer. The owner of the cafe, Denice Sherwin, stops by our table and inquires if our fare is suitably delicious. Silken-haired and petite, clad in an apricot sweater and leggings, she herself looks delicious, and Peleg swivels in his chair to pay her full attention.

Raised a Mormon, she has turned in her maturity to diverse forms of prayer. Her hospitality is the fruit of her spiritual life. Sherwin pauses in her rounds to chime in that prayer is a matter of clarity. "If you set your intention firmly enough, your prayer will be answered." Her intention in founding the cafe was to offer food that was both nutritious and nurturing. Her regular clientele—Peleg included—is grateful for her care.

"I didn't grow up praying—not at all," Peleg tells me. "I grew up in Israel where there was a division between the religious and the secular. I was secular, the child of refugees. One from the Holocaust. My household was one that had lost faith. Prayer wasn't even on the radar."

As a teacher and poet, he paused often.

"I didn't get taught about God, but there was a sense of God that was never taught. Still, you needed to believe in something called God. You didn't have a choice. Your culture had God 'out there.'

"As a youth, I understood a concept of an authoritarian God. Others spoke of God in a fearful way, but I didn't pick up on it. It didn't make sense to me."

Peleg paused, stirring his oatmeal, spooning down a mouthful, then he went on. "In my early thirties I began a practice of prayer as intentional gratitude. I realized that I needed to redefine what prayer meant. Up 'til then it came from a needy place, a place of lack. And so I practiced gratitude, but it wasn't until many years later that I called it prayer. I later realized this is what prayer is about, 'noticed goodness.'"

Peleg ladled some sliced banana into his oatmeal, then continued. "I started making a gratitude list. I kept a journal relating to the law of attraction—like attracts like—bringing my intention to acknowledging good. It became a way to connect to my 'higher self,' a direct channel to connect to God—which we all want, we all crave, even atheists."

Peleg ate a spoonful of banana, then continued, "It's a powerful exercise, acknowledgment. It's hard to receive, yet when people are acknowledged, they come alive. They want to love more and give more. When I acknowledge the universe, I receive it."

Peleg spooned down the last of his oatmeal.

"Delicious," he pronounced with satisfaction. Then he spoke on. "I believe in higher forces—an energetic force that exists. Man didn't invent a tree or a bird. I say to prove there is a God you need only look at a flower, a peach. It's an energetic force of creation. I explored many religions, but organized religion always felt limiting to me. So I practice spirituality, not religion. It's open-ended. It's nice to visit a church or synagogue, but my practice is my own."

It is beginning to snow as I pilot my car back up the mountain, and I know that chances are high that I won't venture out again today. A neighbor has decked green and silver lights above his entryway. They cheer me homeward through the heavy flakes, and I dread the day they will come down. And yet, Santa Fe is slow to shed its finery. Last year some Christmas lights stayed lit until Easter. By the time they came down, spring was in the offing and fruit trees blossomed to replace the lights.

Musing on the beauty of my city, I answered a ringing phone. The caller was my friend Ezra Hubbard, phoning his greetings from sunny southern Florida.

"Ez, I'm getting snowed in again," I told him.

"Snow!" he exclaimed. "What I would give to see snow right now. It's beautiful and hushed, isn't it."

"Well, yes," I reluctantly allowed.

"And you have a treadmill if you get too restless."

"Well, yes," I allowed again.

"That's great! Is the snow sparkling?"

"Well, yes," I allowed once again. Clearly Ezra wasn't going to go along with my scenario. "Poor little Julie. Housebound!"

"Here it's all palm trees," Ezra interjected. He pronounced "palm trees" with palpable disgust. I told him about my piñon tree with its snow-laden branches. He sighed. "Piñon trees. I miss them."

Clearly Ezra and I were at odds, both yearning to swap climates. We both might benefit from a focus on gratitude for what we had rather than what we had not.

"It's always greener on the other side," Ezra concluded. "Enjoy the snow for me."

We got off the phone with terms of endearment. "Dear little Julie. Dear little Ezra." I looked out the window to the piñon tree gently discarding its mantle of white. In its place, I pictured a palm tree, shivering in the chill. Maybe the glorious blue and white day was one to be appreciated. I called to little Lily who had ventured out, placing fresh paw prints in the snow.

"Lily, here, girl," I caroled. She scampered through her dog door and stood looking at me expectantly.

"A good day, isn't it, girl," I breathed.

◄ TRY THIS ►

If we believe in a listening God—and I do—we believe, too, that God has ears for a grateful heart. Making out our gratitude list, we enumerate our blessings from the petty to the profound. "Gratitude is an attitude," goes spiritual wisdom, and as we turn our minds and hearts toward gratitude, we find our attitude brightens. Nudged to the positive, we find ourselves moved to optimism. If, as we are so often taught, God is love, then our loving, grateful hearts move us closer to God. When we are grateful, we discover deeper stores of gratitude. Our numerous blessings build one upon another.

The fastest route to believing in the goodness of the universe is that tried and true exercise: the gratitude list. When I am in a place of needing to connect to my own gratitude, I make it a practice of writing out ten blessings—or gratitudes—every day after I finish Morning Pages.

Quickly fill in the following:

I'm grateful that . . .

I'm grateful that . . .

I'm grateful that . . .

I'm grateful that . . .

I'm grateful that . . .

I'm grateful for . . .

I'm grateful for . . .

I'm grateful for . . .

I'm grateful for . . .

I'm grateful for . . .

I'm grateful for . . .

BOUNTIFUL GRATITUDE

One more time, writing of gratitude, the place to start is with the natural world. The warming moon rises over the mountains. Light washes the courtyard. An hour earlier, the sun set in silken ribbons: fuchsia, topaz, orange, gold. The sun's show was spectacular, ushering in the nighttime sky with its sparkling stars. Gratitude is the attitude that fills my heart. I am grateful for all of the creator's pyrotechnics. Sunset, moonrise, beauty abounding, the heart leaps up. The natural world invites gratitude. What other response is possible? "Praise the Lord," the soul sings. Praise and gratitude dwell side by side, praise occasioning gratitude and gratitude occasioning praise.

The natural world is magnificent, but gratitude can rise up out of homelier roots. First of all, we are grateful that we live, that we draw breath upon breath. Our health is a wonder, our body's intricate systems working in harmony. Each day's march fills us with gratitude. We have a dwelling place, a roof over our heads. We have food and much of it is delicious. If we are lucky—and we often are—we have a pet to keep us company. Its unconditional love fills our hearts. For many of us, our livelihood brings joy. We finish each day awash in gratitude for our productivity. Speaking for myself, I take to the page daily, happy in my work, grateful to have a calling and grateful, at day's end, to have answered that call.

Our friendships are another call for gratitude. Steadfast and loyal, our friends accompany us through life, blessing us with their insights and generosity. My friend Gerard keeps tabs on me long distance. We have been friends for fifty-four years. He weathers my ups and downs with stalwart good humor. I am grateful for his clear-eyed, clearheaded companionship. I jot him cards to tell him of my gratitude.

My sister Libby reminds me of the joy and gratitude to be found in hobbies. She makes mosaics and each tiny chip brings her joy. My sister Lorrie, a master chef, heaps my plate high with gratitude. Her offerings are delicious. My sister Pegi gathers glorious bouquets from her garden. My brothers Jaimie and Christopher make music, filling their lives with melody and gratitude for melody.

You pray in your distress and in your need; would that you might pray also in the fullness of your joy and in your days of abundance.

—KAHLIL GIBRAN

And so we count our blessings, our friends, our families, the abundance we each experience in our unique way. "Gratitude is an attitude," spiritual sages teach us and so, tutored to count our blessings, we find our lives abundant—and we are grateful.

CHECK IN

How many days this week did you do your Morning Pages? Seven out of seven, we hope!

Did you take an Artist Date? What was it? Did you feel an increased connection to your Higher Power during the date? Afterward?

Did you take your walks? What insights bubbled to the fore?

Did you try asking for guidance in writing, and then listening to the answer? What guidance did you receive? Did you try applying it? What surprised you?

PRAYERS
OF
PRAISE

This week we will focus on a third type of prayer: the prayer of praise. We will praise God's gifts—in nature, our fellows, and ourselves—and we will praise Good Orderly Direction, in our lives and in our world. When we look for miracles, we tend to find them. When we become open to co-creating with our creator, support appears. The universe is living and breathing, as we are—and it is responsive to our needs. We seek, and we find that we are partnered at every step. God's blessings are our own. This week, we will celebrate God's gifts. We will actively discover—and rejoice in—the miracles in our lives.

SINGING GOD'S PRAISE

The setting sun gilds the mountain peaks. The sky to the west is striped with fuchsia and gold. The day was spectacularly pretty: bright blue sky, white puffy clouds. It was warmer today than it has been and little Lily ventured out for longer jaunts. The piñon tree hosted a bevy of tiny birds. A lone raven swooped in circles, jubilant on the wind. As the sun sets, the moon rises. It is just past full and still dominates the nighttime sky. Hosannah in the highest, the moon and neighboring stars declare. The natural world sings God's praise.

In cities, the night sky balances atop skyscrapers. The urban lights rival the stars for our attention. And yet, and still, we praise the creator. Man's ambitions reach heavenward. They glitter against the sky.

Ô, Sunlight! The most precious gold to be found on Earth.

—ROMAN PAYNE

Our city canyons invite our notice—and our praise. The marvels of man's making humble the heart. The same moon that rises over the mountains of Santa Fe rises over New York's Empire State Building. The Chrysler Building, with its silvery crown, shouts an alleluia to the sky. Seen from above, our cities are great silver rivers. The lights below seem as miraculous as the stars above.

It is all hosannah. It is all prayer. Man's inventions echo God's ingenuity. The majestic ocean liners on the dark seas, the silvery airliners in the dark skies, these things and more take away our breath as we marvel at their scope and power. Surely God inspired their makers.

From the pyramids to the ruins of Machu Picchu, man's constructions point us back to God. The glory of the Sistine Chapel speaks to us of the creator. On bended knee or not, our souls leap up. "Glory to God in the Highest," we breath our prayer. "And on earth, peace to men of goodwill."

Our goodwill comes to us as we marvel at creation. When we are worshipfully beholding the moon or focusing our awe on a lofty skyscraper, we experience the hush that comes to us as we appreciate God's handiwork and our own. Man's aspirations have their roots in God's inspiration. Marveling at the creator, we become marvels ourselves.

◄ TRY THIS ►

Every time I see the full moon, I say "Thank you, God." And every time I see a new moon, I say, "Oh, thank you, God." The phases of the moon strike me as miraculous—particularly the beginning and the end.

Consciously allow yourself to marvel at the world around you. Put pen to page and list ten people, places, or things that fill you with awe.

WITNESSING THE MIRACULOUS

As I spoke with friends and colleagues about their experience with prayer, a common storyline emerged: a person was brought up in a certain practice, they questioned it, sometimes breaking away, and went on a search for a God of their understanding. Over and over, they reported events—positive, perhaps miraculous events—that showed them they were on the right path for them. My story mirrored the same: I got sober, found my own Higher Power, and saw a way forward as an artist that would work for me—and for others—for decades to come. Stories as old as time speak of spiritual seekers experiencing something that makes them "believe." I believe this can happen for all of us, with each story as unique as the individual at the center of it.

G. Sterling Zinsmeyer, successful producer of film, stage, and opera, eased his way into a corner booth at Santa Fe Bar & Grill. A handsome man with a twinkling smile, he was dressed casually in a blue sweater, tan slacks, and a corduroy jacket. He doffed his jacket as he took his seat, settling in comfortably, prepared for a long conversation on prayer.

Sterling sipped at his Coke, then recalled, "I was schooled in the Catholic trinity—but I found the church very hypocritical. My mother was divorced and she was shunned and shamed by the church—and she was the best Catholic I knew. I knew I was gay from age four, although I didn't have the language for it. I accepted me but the church didn't. I didn't say much, but I was an angry kid.

"My thoughts and my rage over being abandoned by my natural father also weren't acceptable to the church. I kept up Catholic actions, taking solace in receiving communion, but I had many questions—objections—to the liturgy. The turning point for me was my first sexual experience. How could this be a mortal sin?"

"Finished" with the Catholic church, young Sterling went on an eclectic spiritual search, a blend of Tibetan Buddhism and Christianity. But it was the AIDS epidemic that drove him deeper. He recounted what was for him a spiritual awakening. "I was involved in the Buddy program in 1982. This was when I really learned to pray. The spiritual experience of being with someone dying, holding them in your arms, confirmed that there was a universal spiritual energy."

He spoke softly as he remembered, "I felt so significant and insignificant at the same time. All I prayed for was to be centered and be a comfort to the people I was with." By encountering the humanity of others, Sterling encountered his own. He saw himself as part of a greater whole. No longer isolated, he was able to see a way forward in connection and grace.

THE ANVIL OF the epidemic forged for Sterling a spiritual path, a path of service. He began a practice of meditation every morning, ending the session by "asking the divine to let me be of service and kindness on the planet, to turn my actions into prayer." Sterling paused, then explained, "Prayer isn't just asking; it's demonstrating love, kindness, and tolerance."

Sterling came to believe in a spiritual path of his own devising. "I believe in whatever holds up exploding galaxies, that energy, that consciousness, that miraculous force."

Pamela Thompson, life coach, knelt to talk about prayer. Known to her friends as "Pretty Pamela," she wore a blue cashmere sweater, blue fuzzy leggings, and "funny slippers" that featured rhinestones and skulls. She spoke from her home office, a snug space that featured a bed, a desk, and the paintings of her fiancé, Todd Christiansen. Her little dog Louie kept her company.

We find that our thinking will, as time passes, be more and more on the plane of inspiration. We come to rely upon it.

—BILL WILSON

"Yes, I prayed as a child," she said softly. "I was raised Roman Catholic but my father was a Lutheran, so I went to both churches. I prayed for all the kids in the world who were starving, crying as I prayed—I really felt connected. But as a child I was beaten and molested by an uncle, and it made me angry and jaded. 'How could God let that happen?' I demanded."

Pamela's voice grew softer still as she recalled, "My childhood God was big, powerful, sixty feet tall, a guy in the sky with a white beard. He was not doing a great job. If God were all-powerful, how could such bad stuff be happening? I was angry with God for a long time."

Over time, Pamela's rage abated as she worked very hard to heal herself. She enjoyed a greater feeling of peace with God—and then catastrophe struck. "My husband was diagnosed with cancer when we'd only been married five months. The rage at God came back."

When her husband suffered and died, Pamela turned to alcohol to medicate her grief. Her drinking got out of hand and she sought help. Help brought her far more than she bargained for. She joined a spiritual program and had "a miracle shift in perception," seeing that her "perception was off, upside down, and backwards." Realizing that she had power to "clean up her side of the street," she came to peace with God and her tortured past. "A miracle," she exclaimed.

"My uncle was the hardest to forgive, but I saw that if I held on to the hatred, I'd drink. Over one very long weekend, I prayed and prayed. I imagined him as a newborn baby, and that I was holding him in my arms. I saw that he became who he became because of what had been done to him. I felt forgiveness. I'd been told dragons slept with eyes open, and that had been me—but I slept that night with both eyes closed. There was such peace—it was like I could feel the hatred lifted off of me. The next day I got a phone call: 'Your uncle died last night in his sleep.'"

Pamela sighed deeply. She continued her journey. "The course in miracles states, 'The holiest place on earth is where an ancient hatred becomes a present love.'"

It's a matter of discipline for her to strive to be better, more spiritually centered.

Praying now as she travels through her days, Pamela explained, "I pray when driving, when stepping over a threshold. I've gotten down on my knees in a public bathroom. I just can't live without God's presence. I talk to God like I talk to you. An ant prays like an ant. A flower prays like a flower. I pray like a human. I can't live without this connection." Getting to her feet, she concluded, "I've been in some of the darkest places. It is a miracle now to be in the light."

DAVID CAMPBELL LOZUAWAY-MCCOMSEY—"CAMPBELL" to his friends—rose to his feet when I entered Love Yourself Cafe. A genial smile wreathed his face, tilting his mustache. He wore a jaunty blue cap over closely cropped hair. His navy blue sweater, teal slacks, and Xero moccasins were jaunty as well. A big man, barrel-chested, he had a firm handshake.

"I owe it to my mother. She insisted on it." Newly arrived in Santa Fe after a lifetime in New Hampshire, he was, at thirty, enrolled at St. John's College, a school he had dropped out of at twenty-one. With lively green eyes and a ready smile, he hunched over the tiny table, ordering oatmeal topped with coconut whipped cream.

"Mmm," he announced. "I'm glad I asked for the whipped cream." He had a Cheshire cat smile. He began his story. "I grew up in a very open house. I remember we went to the Unitarian Church about ten times. My mother doesn't like the patriarchy of Christianity. When I was in second grade, Mom had a Native American woman named Grey Wing who taught us a prayer to nature. But that's the only prayer I remember from my childhood."

And so, largely untutored in spiritual matters, Campbell passed through his teens. He remembered a turning point. "The first time I prayed I was twenty years old. I was at college, intending to drop out, living an ascetic lifestyle, sleeping with a blanket on the floor. I was on my bed, reading Erich Fromm's *The Art of Being*. He was talking about God and love and I got on my knees on the bed. I asked, "God, who are you? What is love?" I was stricken by the most powerful feeling I ever felt. I started weeping on my bed. I said aloud to myself, 'Campbell, no matter what happens, you know that God is real.'"

Campbell stirred his oatmeal, blending in the whipped cream. He explained, "I felt so much energy in all my limbs and body. I thought of God as love, and love is an energy. I feel like I know less now than I did then."

Determined to make his way as a spiritual seeker, Campbell dropped out of college. For the next four years, his learning was in the school of hard knocks. Turning to pot and alcohol, he thought at first that his spiritual life got better. He became a daily user, and for a time felt happier, more himself. He wrote poems and short stories on drugs. He pursued enlightenment in the bottle—but the bottle soon turned on him.

"When I was handcuffed in a state trooper cruiser for driving drunk, I had a moment of clarity that this nightmare could finally end."

Ordered by the court to have an alcohol and drug evaluation, he was given a choice—get sober or go to jail. He chose sobriety, staying sober under a blanket of fear that he had to answer to the state. He was at risk of drinking again but he was afraid to drink, afraid of going to jail. And the state was watching closely. As part of his treatment plan he had to do a retreat in Amethyst House, a

When man is with God in awe and love, then he is praying.

—KARL RAHNER

sober house, for two days and two nights, learning more about alcoholism. "They said 'make a plan,'" or he would drink, Campbell related his breakthrough. "I did as I was told . . . but I was very angry and in pain."

Fate—or God—intervened again. Campbell ran into Ryan, a man he used to drink with. He admitted to Ryan he needed more structure—or else he knew he would drink. The very next day, Campbell encountered a "sixty-year-old man with twinkly blue eyes," who spoke of a structured recovery plan. Campbell laughed, recalling their encounter. "I chased him down." The older man, Lenny, said he would be "honored" to mentor him, helping Campbell begin an "almost constant practice of prayer." Almost five years later, Lenny is still Campbell's mentor. A miracle, indeed.

JACOB NORDBY, SPIRITUAL writer and life guide, leaned back on a leather couch, resting his stockinged feet on a coffee table. A muscular, bearded man with sparkling gray-blue eyes, he was dressed casually in a long-sleeved midnight-blue shirt, a Christmas gift from his mother, and black sweatpants. His living room was warm and cozy with a large fireplace, oversized mirror, and putty-colored walls featuring candlesticks and an oil painting of the Sawtooth mountains. Resting on his mantlepiece was a shaman's feather from a red-tailed hawk. The scent of sage drifted in the air. A relaxed and humorous man, he turned to the topic of prayer with enthusiasm. His tone turned serious as he recalled a rigid childhood.

"The God I was introduced to as a child was quite punitive. I remember that I would lie awake, as young as four or five, worrying that I might not go up on the rapture if Jesus came over," Jacob began his story.

"We prayed a lot at home and at church. I was taught to pray at bed every night. It was enforced," he continued gravely. "At eight or nine I was made to do devotions, reading a chapter of the Bible, praying by myself. It was a nightly obligation.

"We were taught that those who weren't saved would stay on earth to have punishments from other sinners and the devil. The devil was a force nearly as powerful as God. He was very personal—trying to trick us into sin to spite God and damn us into hell."

Jacob paused, his voice thickening as he remembered his tormented young self. "I tried hard to be a true believer. I was quite compliant. At the same time, I was having mystical experiences of God, a different God, that I couldn't explain. I remember looking up at a pine tree and experiencing pure joy. But when I tried to talk of it, I was told to get back in line."

Growing older, Jacob experienced still more doubt. He was struggling to believe what he was taught and he was increasingly revolted by the message. His twenties were a time of turmoil as he sought to repress his true feelings and conform to the church's expectations. Stuffing his true nature, he gained seventy pounds, successful but miserable in an entrepreneurial career. He founded several companies, purchased a large and impressive home, and buried his spiritual longings in work and overwork.

Then came a dramatic turning point. "I was thirty-four. I had been away from the church for ten years, spiritually seeking, finding some comfort in New Age readings. I encountered, in glimpses, a peaceful God—not punitive. I remember weeping to imagine God in ways that weren't frightening."

Jacob paused again, stretching to a more comfortable posture as he recalled, "A young man came to work at one of my companies. He took me on a meditation retreat in a mountain town. I went, feeling afraid and anxious—yet to go felt important to me. I got there and found it was a shamanic retreat. I didn't know what a shaman was.

The most beautiful moments in life are moments when you are expressing your joy.

—JAGGI VASUDEV

"I experienced what felt like a miracle to me—I saw the word 'love' written in the sky. I realized—in a moment—that everything is made of love, there is no fear in love, that perfect love casts out fear. In a split second I saw that I was not alone, I was made of God, a part of God that could never be separated. I saw an image of me as a man—overweight and out of shape—but I felt held and loved and accepted as never before. I didn't know how to bring my physical life into alignment with this freedom, joy, love, and power, but the desire was a starting point. That changed everything."

Jacob's dramatic experience was a turning point for him. Perhaps his mystical experiences as a child had primed him for the moment. Perhaps he had just reached a breaking point and needed to move in a new direction. Perhaps his time doubting God prepared him for a sudden flash of clarity. Everyone's path is different, and spiritual awakenings come in many shapes and sizes.

Jacob curled his legs beneath him. It was late afternoon and the winter's light through the window was growing dim. He leaned forward and continued, "That was twelve years ago, and since then it has been a process of coming home to heal. Take prayer. I was put off of prayer by virtue of my upbringing. When I began writing Morning Pages, I began to be honest and simply admit out loud, on paper, that I had needs. That felt like the beginning of a prayer. And then, gradually, I began a practice of writing out guidance. I would write something and I would hear something back. The answer was always gentle and peaceful. I would sometimes think, 'Is this too good to be true?' but I never got scolded for my doubts. The 'voice' welcomed me. That began dissolving the barrier of prayer for me."

These days Jacob has a regular practice of prayer. "It's very conversational. Sometimes I speak and whisper aloud for guidance and help." Moving through his day, he finds himself praying often. "When I'm driving or waiting in a line, I'll find myself irritated, and then I'll remember to pray and I'll find myself again at peace."

Over time, Jacob's concept of God has shifted and grown. "My childhood God was male, insecure, perfectionistic, easily angered, always looking for wrongs and faults. My God now is loving—inescapably loving—gentle, wise but practical, peaceful, intimate . . . like a best friend who cannot be offended."

◄ TRY THIS ►

When I got sober, I built a new relationship with a Higher Power as well as a new relationship to my own creativity. I realized that they were connected—so connected that I often say they are one and the same. When I am asked about the most powerful spiritual turning point in my life, it is this. I have lived, taught, and created based on these principles ever since.

Fill in the following:

The most powerful experience of my life to date was _____.

I felt the hand of God when _____.

I believe I had a spiritual experience when _____.

I felt closest to God when _____.

It is possible that a higher force was at play when _____.

Some of us have dramatic spiritual experiences, while some of us experience the miracles of the world in more subtle ways. All are valid. All are powerful. Fill in the following:

(cont'd)

> A dramatic miracle I have experienced is . . .
>
> A subtle miracle I have experienced is . . .
>
> An element of nature that I find miraculous is . . .

A NEW YEAR

New Year's Day dawned blue and silver. The snow glistened in the early morning light. It has been cold, too cold for the snow to melt, and so the white blanket remains. I woke late from a dream of dolphins. In my dream, I heard two dolphins talking about the human race. The dolphins were saying, "We know they're smart. We just don't know how smart." I laughed aloud.

The day was quiet. No phone shrilled. I padded to the kitchen to feed my little dog and make coffee. Despite my good night's sleep, I was tired and grumpy. The year opened with a cranky mood. Taking to the page, I sipped coffee and wrote my three Morning Pages. One mug, two mugs, three mugs of coffee, and I was finally awake and alert. A wave of anxiety nipped at me and I took to the page a second time, writing out a prayer.

"Please lift my mood. Please give me good cheer." Writing the prayer, invoking divine aid, I could feel my mood lifting. Blessings, after all, surrounded me—my snug house, my courtyard glittering with snow, a lovely sight. With my mood lifting, I decided to call my friend Emma Lively, a near constant source of optimism and joy.

"Happy New Year, Emma," I wished her when she answered.

"Happy New Year," she echoed.

A morning is a wonderful blessing. It stands for hope, giving us another start of what we call Life.

—UNKNOWN

"It's cold and clear and snowy here," I told her. My voice crackled. It hadn't been used.

"Are you drinking water?" Emma wanted to know. She was always after me to drink more water.

"Some," I allowed.

"Drink more," she advised. "Go get some now."

Obedient, I again padded to the kitchen, retrieving an icy bottle of water from the refrigerator.

"I'm back," I announced into the phone. "Did you stay up until midnight last night?"

"No. I'm afraid not. I went to bed early and got a good night's sleep."

Emma was in rehearsals for her musical, *Bliss,* which was opening soon in Seattle. Her days were long; up at five, at the studio by eight, working a twelve-hour day. She was short on sleep and running on adrenaline. New Year's was a day off and a welcome opportunity to sleep in. My call caught her and her co-creator, Tyler Beattie, hard at work on last-minute rewrites. She was good-tempered about my interruption. Tyler's piano tinkled in the background. "He's working out a transition," Emma explained.

"I stayed up," I told Emma. "I talked to Jacob Nordby and wrote."

"On your book?" Emma asked.

"No. About the year past and the year to come."

"Ah-hah."

"2019 was a good year for writing, but I think the new year will be even better. I'm enjoying my writing right now."

"That's great."

"Emma, I'll let you get back to work. I'll talk to you later," I signed off. The day loomed empty ahead of me.

"I'll just hop on the treadmill," I thought. Taking a journal from the fall with me, I climbed onto the machine. I was curious to read how I had been feeling for the several months prior. The days had been crammed with travel and teaching. Except for Morning Pages, I wasn't current with myself. Setting a low grade and a slow pace, I began to walk and read. My pages were filled with prayers and requests for guidance.

The guidance was there, too, and it was vastly reassuring. "You are on track. You are led carefully and well," I was told repeatedly. "Your plays will find homes," I was assured. Turning the pages of my season past, I found the tone of the guidance to be gentle but firm. "There is no need for anxiety," I was repeatedly scolded. That, and "write."

Confronted with that directive, I had written. The pages of the prayer book had mounted up. In just six weeks, I had accumulated a third of a book. My fears of the topic—prayer—had largely abated. The guidance had this to say about that: "Do not fear running out of ideas. We will inspire you."

The "we" was what I had come to call "Higher Forces." Angels? Saints? "We are happy to remain anonymous." Speaking through my own hand as I wrote, Higher Forces repeatedly assured me, "You are in our custody. You are in our care."

Reading the gentle admonishments, I felt myself relaxing. "There is no need for anxiety." A step at a time, a page at a time, I felt myself growing in faith. The guidance had led me through a hectic and busy season. It was surefooted and kind.

Stepping off the treadmill, I thought, "Now I'll write." Settling onto the love seat, I took pen in hand. Reviewing my notes, I put pen to the page, writing up a particularly complex interview. It was my plan to interview a dozen or more subjects, exploring the depth and breadth of their prayer lives.

To date, the people I interviewed agreed on one thing:

prayer was a central part of their lives. Ranging from Baptist to Catholic, from Buddhist to Hindu, they were all in agreement that prayer was a "conversation" they couldn't live without. Their conceptions of God varied from an "energy" to a "best friend" to a "benevolent something." But they all agreed on two points: God was real, and we could contact God. That conscious contact was made through prayer.

As I concentrated on my work, the day sped past. Soon it was time to head out the door to meet with friends. We were just days past the winter solstice, and the day was still short. As I piloted my car down the mountain and into town, I passed many houses still bedecked with Christmas lights. They lifted my heart, and I found myself speaking a prayer out loud. "Thank you, God," I prayed each time I passed a gloriously lit home. There were angels, stars, Santas, and nativity scenes. All spoke of the sacred season. "Thank you, God," I breathed aloud.

After dinner with friends, I drove back up the mountain, passing more and more occasions for prayer.

Piloting my car into the garage, I opened the door to my house and was greeted cheerfully by Lily.

"Hello, sweet pea," I crooned. She leapt up, planting her paws on my legs. Her tail wagged gaily. Tousling her snowy coat, I pulled away, crossing the kitchen to check on her food and water—both full.

One more time, I retreated to the love seat. I picked up my journal and wrote, "January 1—later." I recorded my better mood. It had been a good day after all. Productive. Putting aside my journal, I went down the hall to my bedroom where I changed into pajamas. Happy New Year.

◄ **TRY THIS** ►

Look back and read through the guidance you have
written over the past weeks. Read the questions you
had asked, and the answers you received. Was your
guidance prescient, wise, encouraging, helpful?
In retrospect, what do you see? Have your questions changed? Have your feelings about what you
"hear" evolved over this time? Do you find yourself
more willing to trust your guidance than you were
when you began?

IN GOD'S TIME

It is a crisp, blue day. The snow has melted atop the
mountains and they are once again green. Fir trees climb
their heights. "Thank you, God," I breathe, "for giving us
a break in winter." Surely more snow will come, but until
it does it's nice to pretend spring is just around the corner. This has been a cold and snowy season. Muffled in
a winter coat and scarf and hat, I trudge through the icy
days. At nightfall, temperatures drop into the teens. It's
easy to argue with God about the weather. Cranky from
the cold, it is easy to argue with God, period. Rebellion
seizes the heart.

"My will, not thine," we want to pray. If, in fact, we
can be said to pray at all. Grace is the comfortable feeling
of alignment with God. Our position now is adversarial.
God's will strikes us as harsh and punitive. We take issue
with it, feeling ourselves to be bullied. God is a thug, we
think to ourselves. God's will runs counter to our desires.

Sensing that to fight with God is futile, we nonethe-
less persist. We are picking a fight over all the many times
we have felt thwarted. "And what about X?" we demand,

unwilling or unable to accept that God was acting on our own behalf.

It is said there are three answers to prayer: "yes," "no," and "not now." Fighting with God over what seems to be a prevalence of negatives, we are unable to recall to mind a time of answered prayer. No matter that God's will has seen in cozy retrospect to be benevolent. At the moment, we have no long view. We have asked God for a reasonable something and, we feel, we have been unreasonably denied. "And it will always be this way," we mutter. This fight with God will persist into eternity.

We know our battle to be futile but we wage our battle of wills. We feel ourselves to be unfairly bludgeoned. God is Goliath and we are puny Davids. God towers all-powerful and, we feel, unreasonable. Dimly, in some small part of ourselves, we sense that our argument with the creator is a losing proposition. We do know that God is almighty and that our only reasonable action is surrender.

"Oh, all right!" we fume, bending our will to God's. The fight has left us exhausted. God is, of course, the victor as we relinquish our stubborn will. "Thy will be done," we mumble, noting as we do a sense of relief. "It is better to be on God's side," we conclude. We will find that the timing of many things is not our choice at all, and in surrendering, we are free.

I received a call today from my friend Daniel Region. He wanted to ask me, "When will spring come?" He explained, "We had an early winter. Maybe we'll have an early spring."

"We'll see about that," I told him, knowing better than to second-guess God's timing. Still, I sympathized with Daniel and his desire to dictate to God. If there was one arena in which we frequently fought with God, it was the arena of timing. We argued with God over big

We don't want to wait for God to resolve matters in His good time because His idea of "good time" is seldom in sync with ours.

—OSWALD CHAMBERS

things—the seasons—and small: the arrival of a long-awaited paycheck. No matter that in retrospect God's timing was always perfect. Spring, when it came, was always welcome. So, too, the paycheck. God's timing was always impeccable, taking into account variables visible only to divine eyes.

Daniel and I make a plan to get together. He lives in Albuquerque, an hour's drive from me in Santa Fe. We will meet in three weeks' time, just after my trip to Seattle to teach and to view *Bliss*, my friend Emma's musical. Three weeks seem like a long time to wait for a visit but lately time has seemed speeded up. Human time coming closer to God's. "Three weeks, then," I tell Daniel.

Much has been written about God's sense of time. We have been told repeatedly that God lives in eternity and eternity is timeless, one long "now." God's sense of "soon" may therefore differ from our own. Awaiting word on my plays, I have been told that I need patience. Told that I will have "good tidings soon," I chafe at the bit, impatient. God's "soon" is not soon enough for me.

"Pray for acceptance of God's timing," I am told and so I try it. To my surprise, I feel a lessening of urgency. Prayer works! One more time, I use the serenity prayer. The thing I "cannot change" is God's timing. The thing I can change is my attitude toward it. Bowing to the Higher Power, I sense a release. No longer agitated or fretful, I resolve to cooperate with divine timing. I will wait, trusting that God knows best.

This trust is built on past experience. This is not the first time I have wanted God to hurry up. And what happened? When God's timing came around, I myself had to rush to be in sync with it. I wasn't as "ready" as I thought.

God's timing is a lot like cooking. Each variable—each dish—must be properly timed to go with the others. The perfect meal is the result of skill and experience. God's sweet potatoes take longer than God's biscuits. And the

Blessed is the soul that can recognize that he isn't moving mountains, but God is for him.

—SHANNON ALDER

pies can bake along with the turkey. The result of careful planning is delicious. And so, too, is God's timing, perfect in retrospect—delicious.

Spring will come when spring comes. I will hear about my plays when I hear about my plays. In the interim I will look for the silver lining. A long, cold winter is perfect for writing. Another play can be written while I wait upon my plays. And so the answer to Daniel's query "When will spring come?" is very simply "When God wills it."

◄ TRY THIS ►

Recall a time when God's timing—not your own—turned out to be the best timing. Fill in the following sentences:

I remember when I wanted God to hurry up and _____.

Instead, _____ happened when _____.

In retrospect, this timing was _____.

It was better for me in that I _____.

I was protected when _____.

Now, fill in the following:

In retrospect, God's timing was perfect when . . .

In retrospect, God's timing was perfect when . . .

In retrospect, God's timing was perfect when . . .

In retrospect, God's timing was perfect when . . .

In retrospect, God's timing was perfect when . . .

A FAMILY OF CHOICE

We are all born into families and communities, and raised within the values of the people around us. As we become more and more independent, we question more, and all of us, to some degree, go on a search for our own truth. We expand our circles, choosing friends, colleagues, and partners who we will build our lives with. Sometimes we are led to circles that very much mirror our upbringing. And sometimes, we choose to build a life that stands in contrast to the one we were born into. For most of us, our lives become a combination of both. For some of us, the search is an arduous one. Each of us, open to being guided on our path, has the power to find our "family of choice."

Genial and gentle, tall and lean, Scott Thomas, healer and psychologist, edged his lanky frame into a corner booth at The Red Enchilada.

For thirty years a practitioner of psychology and ceremonies, blending a distinguished education with his own Native Lakota traditions, he was prepared to talk on prayer—which was central to his personal life and professional practice. His business card laid out some of his path. It read "Scott Thomas, PhD," and, following his name, a long stream of initials: LCSW, LADAC, CDVC.3. Deciphered, they meant he was a licensed clinical social worker, a licensed alcoholism and drug addiction counselor, and a certified domestic violence counselor. He wore his credentials lightly, as casually as he was dressed in a striped shirt, denim jacket, tan slacks, and sneakers, his hair in a neat braid.

Ordering a bowl of beans with green chili and onions, he sipped on hot water and lemon. Asked if he prayed as a child, he said, "Oh, yes. We prayed every day to survive. My father was a violent alcoholic." After a beat, he elaborated. "My mom was very Catholic and I went to Catholic church and Sunday school."

What he learned there was of little help to him, but parallel to the Catholic liturgy were the beliefs of his grandparents, Lakota elders. "My grandparents on the reservation always believed in ceremonies and the pipe."

He explained the significance of the pipe. "In all ceremonies everywhere around the world, there are sacred objects which have incredible power to move us and to heal us." The pipe was one such object. "It had the power to signify that we were of like mind and it had the power to give the experience that we were all joined in our relatedness."

Unlike his mother's Catholic prayers, prayers in the Lakota tradition of his grandparents were behavioral. Scott spoke respectfully of what was taught. "It was how you behaved, how you lived your life that counted. There were formal prayers, but your spiritual identity came from how you spoke to and interacted with the people around you."

Speaking slowly and carefully, Scott described a gentle culture, but growing up he found it to be in scary contrast to the violence and alcoholism he was also experiencing. He explained his own descent into alcoholism. "If you're a very sensitive person, sometimes it seems the only way to live is to drink alcohol. Drinking is a protection from getting your feelings hurt every day. Of course that doesn't work, not for long."

From his teen years until he was twenty-four, Scott tried unsuccessfully to use alcohol as a protection, descending into darkness and despair. He remembered the turning point in his young life. "My older family members—aunts, uncles, grandparents—helped me to find myself again through the love of family and the ceremonies that joined us together. My family has always prayed for me and I will always pray for them. We don't always agree but we always pray for each other."

In addition to his family, Scott was intervened upon

When we give cheerfully and accept gratefully, everyone is blessed.

—MAYA ANGELOU

by what he calls his "family of choice. Allies that show up in your life. Special people who love you unconditionally. If someone loves you at your lowest point, it is a defining moment. You will remember it the rest of your life and you will always be different because of it."

Picking up his spoon, Scott took another deep mouthful. It was a cold night and the warmth of the beans and chili felt good. He continued, bridging his two cultures, educated elder and tribal man. "In some circles they call that transformation or a conversion experience."

Calling it his "defining moment," Scott got sober. He names two special mentors, his uncle Sereondo Trujillo "who took an interest," and a kindly woman, Teresa Neimic, who ran a halfway house where he got on his feet. Having been burned himself in the fires of addiction, young Scott resolved that he would help others. But first, he realized he needed "an education in the dominant culture." He enrolled in college at age twenty-six, and after achieving his bachelor's degree, "I just kept going."

As he immersed himself in "the dominant culture," he immersed himself ever more deeply in Lakota tradition, participating fully in the Sundance Ceremony, dancing for four days and four nights from sun up to sun down without food or water. The hardship of the ceremony was a sacrifice offered up "for the good of the world."

Scott sacrificed, too, to obtain his education. Living in a trailer on his uncle's land, he had no electricity, heat, or running water, just a wood stove and a kerosene lamp. "I had the sun and the river, the food I got through hunting and fishing. It was a harsh time, simple, but beautiful."

Living, as his uncle teased him, "like an Indian," Scott sought to connect again with spirits. "If a man is drinking, spirits will still be around him, but they turn their backs and won't look at him." Sober, Scott felt himself closer to spirits and their guidance. Living off the land, washing his body in the river, he felt led to help others. "I wanted to help others because I had been helped."

Scott's education gave him words, many words. His Lakota tradition gave him compassion. His two cultures became integrated in his own psyche. Leading through example, he helped many—on and off the reservation—by virtue of his own sobriety. Meanwhile, he continued his education, gaining degrees and therapeutic expertise. Blending his knowledge of conventional therapeutic practices with his deep belief in Lakota healing techniques, he gradually founded his personal practice specializing in "counseling and healing." Scott listened to the stories of his clients and "led them to their own healing." He combined listening and storytelling, psychology and ceremonies. His practice thrived.

Ladling up a spoonful of beans, Scott spoke of his personal prayer practice, Lakota in its grounding. He explained, "Every morning, I put out a bowl of food and a shot glass of coffee. I offer it to the sun. I name my ancestors and ask for my thoughts, words, and actions to be guided.

"Just because the body is dead, the soul does not evaporate. When the body is gone our soul becomes more available to help others. If we close our eyes and get quiet, we can hear them. Everyone can."

Scott leaned back and raised his arms above his head, palms open. With his silver hair braided in a plait down his back, and his eyes closed, he looked for a moment wholly Lakota. Opening his eyes, dropping his hands, he drew a small leather pouch from around his neck.

"I wear protection," he explained. "The pouch has sage, eagle down, and a small round stone my grandmother gave me when I was young."

Now that he is no longer young, Scott is considered by many to be an elder. His wisdom is soft-spoken but grounding. Setting aside his spoon, Scott finished his meal

You'll never find a rainbow if you're looking down.

—CHARLIE CHAPLIN

and his thoughts on an optimistic note. "You don't have to know the answer to know there is an answer. Once you believe there is an answer, the next step will be revealed."

As I listen to Scott, I reflect that he embodies praise, from his spirit of service to his ceremonial upbringing: for nature, for people, for his ancestors, and for God.

◄ **TRY THIS** ►

All of us have the power to build a "family of choice." Fill in the following:

The people who raised me were supportive about _____.

I lacked support in that _____.

I was able to find that support when _____.

An area where I am still looking for support is _____.

One person I could ask for help is _____.

SYNCHRONICITY

One of the most marvelous and impressive aspects of God is the delightful surprise known as synchronicity. We are often pleasantly astonished by what appear to be unlikely coincidences. Our inner world and our outer world abruptly mesh. The hand of God moves across our life, causing a remarkable "coincidence" to occur. Often, we no sooner clarify a wish than our wish is fulfilled. Synchronicity catches us off guard. We do not really expect the universe to respond so quickly and accurately as it does when synchronicity is at play.

Let us say we realize a desire to do a life drawing. "But how?" we wonder. "I know nothing about life drawing, only that I appreciate the end result." Our wish becomes a yearning, and our yearning is unexpectedly answered when, at a dinner party, we are seated next to a visual artist who teaches beginners.

"I've got one slot left," the artist relays when we dare to speak to him of our desire. "If you want it, it's yours," he tells us. "It would be a delight to have a peer in my class." And so we take the slot and we are excited to learn the rudiments of the life-drawing craft. We say "yes" to opportunity when it presents itself.

Synchronicity requires that we say "yes" in order for its action to be fulfilled. And yet it isn't always easy to give our consent to the universe. Synchronicity may strike us as "too good to be true," and so we will turn the opportunity aside, foiling the good wishes of the Great Creator.

"Just say yes," spiritual teachers advise us. They are alert to the fortuitous opportunities that we are provided. Saying yes, we increase our connection to the divine. Saying yes requires a willing acceptance of synchronicity.

Anything can happen, child.
Anything can be.

—SHEL SILVERSTEIN

And how do we encourage synchronicity to happen in our lives? The most direct route that I have found through years of practice, my own and my students', is to employ the combination of Morning Pages and Artist Dates. We put our desires out into the world in Morning Pages, and the world responds during—and after—Artist Dates. I have often laughed at experiences of synchronicity where it feels like, "Now God's just showing off." I have had students report that materials needed for a project seemed to "magically" appear to them—the perfect couch at a garage sale for the blackbox play, a sale on watercolors just when painting had sounded enticing, a friend-of-a-friend editor offering help just when a book draft was needing a fresh set of eyes.

Working with Morning Pages and Artist Dates over the years, I have found synchronicity to be something I can count on. The Great Creator—our co-creator—wants to help us, after all, and our dreams have come from this higher force. I invite you to experiment with being open to the possibility of this helping hand, and to the signals from the outer world, large and small, that this hand is here to help, indeed.

◄ **TRY THIS** ►

We have all had experiences of synchronicity, large and small. Fill in the following:

1. I was in the right place at the right time when . . .

2. I was in the right place at the right time when . . .

3. I was in the right place at the right time when . . .

1. I felt like I had a "lucky break" when . . .

2. I felt like I had a "lucky break" when . . .

3. I felt like I had a "lucky break" when . . .

1. It's possible that a higher force was helping me when . . .

2. It's possible that a higher force was helping me when . . .

3. It's possible that a higher force was helping me when . . .

1. The thing I'd most like help with now is . . .

2. The thing I'd most like help with now is . . .

3. The thing I'd most like help with now is . . .

Look over your lists. Do you see the mark of a higher hand? Experiment with asking for help, and then be alert to help and support from unlikely quarters.

A MIGHTY STORM

The piñon tree is laden with snow and more snow is falling. Tiny birds take shelter amid its branches and larger birds, braving the storm, flit through the falling flakes to perch on the portal. Early this morning when the storm was just gathering muster, I drove down the mountain for supplies. As I drove back up, my car skidded. The roads were already icy. I piloted the last quarter mile with extreme caution, skidding again as I braked for my drive. Safely garaged, I took note that my car's hood was coated with ice. It was not a day to be driving again. It was a day to be snowbound.

Inside my house, I cranked up the heat to seventy-four. I got a blanket and an extra sweater. My normally snug abode felt chilly. A thick snow fell outside my living room windows. Winter was having its day. Humbled by the storm, I took pen to page, praying for guidance. "Write on humility," I was told.

The storm humbled cars and drivers. The roads, unplowed as yet, were treacherous. I was not alone in skidding. A lone raven flapped overhead as I turned up the mountain. Its caw was belligerent, braving the storm. "Dear God, let me get home safely," I prayed. I had three casseroles stacked on the seat beside me. They would make for tasty but monotonous eating. The storm was predicted to last all day, all night, and into the following day. Its fury bludgeoned the earth. The piñon tree bowed its head, heavy snow burdening its branches.

Curled in my blanket, I placed a call to my friend Nick, canceling our evening's plans. "Yes," Nick said. "I think it's wise. You'll be getting a lot of snow up there on the mountain." Next, I called my friend Barbara, canceling our plan for an afternoon rendezvous. "Yes," Barbara echoed Nick, "I think it's wise. It's snowing like fury. It's better to be safe." I fielded a third call, this one from my daughter, Domenica.

"I'm snowbound," I told her.

"Oh, Mommy," she sympathized.

"I've canceled all my plans, dinner with Nick, an afternoon with Barbara."

"I'm glad you've canceled. I want you to be safe."

"This morning my car skidded."

"Oh, Mommy," she sounded worried.

"I made it home."

"So stay home. You can call me later if you need company." My daughter knew me well.

We hung up the phone, happy to have connected across the miles, despite the storm. Fast and furious flakes were falling. Now the birds abandoned the portal and joined their tiny fellows in the piñon tree's sheltering branches.

"I am mighty," the storm proclaimed, swirling against my windows. I called my friend Jacob who was driving in Boise, a balmy forty-nine degrees.

"I'm snowbound and this morning my car skidded," I complained.

"Goodness. You didn't hit anything, did you?" he asked, worry eddying in his voice.

"No. There was nothing near me," I told him. "But the storm is humbling."

"How so?" he asked.

"'I'm mightier than you and your little cars,' it proclaims."

"Ah, yes. Last night there was a big snow here in Boise and I found myself worrying about the safety of my son driving."

"So you do know what I mean!"

"Yes, I'm afraid so. Winter is my least favorite season."

"The storm is supposed to go all night. I may call you again later if I need company."

"Please do. I'm staying in."

"I'll talk to you later. Good-bye."

Yes, the storm was humbling, evoking prayers for our safety and, in Jacob's case, prayers for the safety of those we love. The humbled heart prays to God the almighty. Humility is always an appropriate response to God. When we are humble, we are right sized, modest before our creator. We do not grovel, for the creator has made us worthy. We approach God with gentle confidence, knowing that as we cherish our connection, we are cherished in return. My guidance comes back to me plainspoken. "I love you," I hear. What could be more direct, more heartwarming than that?

The storm outside swirls on. "Please keep me safe and warm," I pray, trusting that my humble prayer will be answered. The snow announces God's omnipotence, at once ferocious and gentle. Humbled, I stay in.

For me, prayer is a surge of the heart; it is a simple look turned toward heaven, it is a cry of recognition and of love, embracing both trial and joy.

—ST. THERESE OF LISIEUX

THE MOUNTAINS LOOM, green and purple. The sky above them is clear blue. Today there is no snow and the sun is busily at work melting the deep snow that has fallen. My piñon tree shakes its branches in a light breeze. The last of its snowy burden slips to the ground. No ravens scavenge for food. Instead, the small birds emerge, coming out from hiding to greet the sunny day. The drama of the storm has passed, but another drama awaits.

The snow is melting rapidly. My dirt road, unplowed, is a sea of icy slush. As I pilot my car through the muck, a flotilla of ravens swoops across the road. My car doesn't scare them. They allow us passage but nothing more. Their dark wings cast shadows on my windshield. Landing in the road ahead, they strut proudly in twos and threes. Should I honk?

I make the turn into my driveway and press the button for the garage door to slide open. A few bold ravens follow me in, veering skyward at the last moment. Humbled once again, I hurriedly close the door. I enter the house only to be greeted by loud "caws" and ravens flapping by my windows. The ravens are dog-size and little Lily stares out the window apprehensively. She gives a worried "yip" but the ravens' raucous "caws" drown her out.

One more time, the piñon tree is shedding its blanket of snow. The ravens visit its upper branches, making a meal as nuts fall to the ground. Inside the house, I, too, am making a meal: a vegan casserole from Love Yourself Cafe. It features kale, sweet potatoes, onions, zucchini, squash, mushrooms, and, finally, vegan cheese. Lily begs for a morsel, forgetting about the ravens who are quiet now, eating. I have never seen so many ravens at once, and I remind myself that ravens are good luck, the "first animal," in Druidic lore. They are the "totem animal" of my friend Julianna McCarthy. Like the birds, she is bold and daring. At ninety years of age, she lives atop a mountain. She is on the alert for ever-present bears. My mountain has bears, too, but not in winter when they hibernate. They will be back out in spring, giving the ravens something to think about. Giving the human residents something to think about as well—"Bear alert," the word passes neighbor to neighbor. One neighbor, a sort of town crier, adds to the bear alert, "Be careful going into your house." And so I picture a bear hulking at the garage door.

"Dear God," I pray. "Please keep me and the little dog safe. Protect us from ravens and from bears." In the summer, I will add, "And from snakes." I pray to coexist peacefully with the animals on my mountain. After all, I must admit with humility, they were here first.

◄   TRY THIS   ►

When we are at our most humble, we often feel the most aware of a Higher Power. Hitting the bedrock of humility, the utter understanding that we are not in control, allows us to connect with God. Think of the moments when you have felt most humbled by a force greater than yourself, and fill in the following:

I was humbled when . . .

I was humbled when . . .

I was humbled when . . .

I was humbled when . . .

I was humbled when . . .

Now, look at each of your answers. Do you see evidence of the miraculous in any of your experiences? In all of them?

LIFE IS A PRAYER

Every day, I pray for guidance that I may know what to write. I listen for an idea and I write the idea out, trying not to second-guess myself. It is sometimes difficult to have faith, but when I follow the guidance faithfully, I am rewarded.

Late in the afternoon, on a day when I hadn't yet written, I was restless and irritable—two sure signs that I needed to write. Accordingly, I took pen to page and wrote out a request for guidance. I listened for a response and I heard, "Julia, you are in my care. I guard and guide you. You are safe and protected." Before I could listen further, my phone rang. Ezra Hubbard was calling me. I took it to be an answered prayer. Ezra has a vibrant and vital spiritual life. I could tell him I needed an idea to write about prayer.

"Ezra, I'm stuck," I told him. "I haven't written yet today and I need to write. In order to write, I need an idea. Do you have any ideas about prayer?"

"Life is a prayer," Ezra answered promptly. He didn't elaborate. I thought immediately of his palm trees in southern Florida and my fir trees in northern New Mexico. The branches of each reached heavenward. True to their individual natures, they each fulfilled their particular destiny. There was no confusion. They each grew as they were intended to grow. It was God's will that they would each flourish as they did. No questions asked. Simple compliance with divine intent.

Next I thought of the mighty oak trees towering high in New York's Central Park. The giants grew from tiny acorns. It was their destiny to be mighty and they complied. The willow tree bowed its long-haired strands, graceful and sheltering to the mallards that made their home beneath its shade along the shore. Skittering up the trunk of a maple, squirrels cavorted, as was their nature. Their antics caught the attention of a golden retriever passing placidly at its owner's side. Yes, the park was a playground for the buoyant boxer and the silken cocker spaniel. Dogs of all sizes and shapes appeared on the pathways. From the husky to the greyhound, each was true to its breed.

The most beautiful experience we can have is the mysterious. It is the fundamental emotion that stands at the cradle of true art and true science.

—ALBERT EINSTEIN

I thought of the diversity of life, each bit of creation a hosannah. In my garden in Santa Fe, lilacs grew side by side with lilies. Tulips neighbored cacti. All these years later, I still stand by my belief that Dylan Thomas had it right, honoring "the force that through the green fuse drives the flower." The creative energy destined each bud differently. Surely Ezra was right and the diversity—life—was a prayer.

The sky is a serene blue. A few puffy white clouds sail into view. One more time, the temperature is warm. Spring is not yet here, but it is nearing. Walking Lily, I spotted four robins—sure harbingers of the coming season. Lily is grateful for the turn in the weather—it means we can resume our daily walks. There is security in our routine. There is more security in God's routine. Spring will surely follow winter.

At the market, I buy a large bouquet of lilies. They unfold slowly, scenting the house with their aphrodisiac smell. Their heady aroma is yet another signal of approaching spring. I bask in a feeling of security. The flowers promise future flowers to come. I have lilies in my garden, and soon enough they will bloom. The piñon tree is finished with its last season, and it is readying itself for the season yet to come. The ravens have made a last meal of its offerings. A few bold squirrels feed on what the ravens have missed.

On a clear day, such as today, the mountains loom tall and bold. Their upper peaks are snowy. Their lower heights are green with piñon. There is great beauty in the vista. At twilight, the snowy white peaks will turn color, reflecting the sunset. But until then, they are alabaster—radiant in the sunshine, glorious in their pristine beauty.

"Dear God, make your presence known," I pray. And the mountaintops seem to hold a home for the Great Creator. I know that God is everywhere—here below, in the branches of the piñon tree—but my imagination prefers a God of the heights, all seeing. Now a little flotilla of clouds appears, wrapping the mountaintops in gauze. I picture God in human form, with a scarf of clouds wrapped around his neck. The creative energy is benevolent, and regards humankind with compassion. "Dear God, thank you for this beauty," I pray.

Beauty is a gateway to God. Loveliness is next to godliness. A magnificent stag appears in a roadside meadow. Its companion doe follows soon after. At its flank, a petite fawn. The trio sparks joy. A raven swoops overhead, its black wings glistening. A second raven joins its flight. Nature is God's handiwork. A portly raccoon crosses the road. Flora and fauna alike speak of God.

I keep tabs by phone with my far-flung friends. Andrew Franklin in gray London. Emma Lively in cold New York. Scottie Pierce basking in sunny San Diego and, of course, Ezra toiling in his artist's studio in Florida. My friends are diverse but each blossoms in their chosen habitat. They are true to their natures, particular as the flowers in my garden.

"Life is a prayer," Ezra had declared. I see his point. Each plant and person has a divine spark urging it to fulfill its destiny, to add its voice to the mighty chorus that is life.

CHECK IN

How many days this week did you do your Morning Pages? Seven out of seven, we hope!

Did you take an Artist Date? What was it? Did you feel an increased connection to your Higher Power during the date? Afterward?

Did you take your walks? What insights bubbled to the fore?

Did you try asking for guidance in writing, and then listening to the answer? What guidance did you receive? Did you try applying it? What surprised you?

CREATIVITY
AND
SPIRITUALITY

This week, we will explore the link between creativity and spirituality—which has been the base of my teaching and the springboard for my art for the past forty-plus years. If "the force that through the green fuse drives the flower" can work for me as a Higher Power, and if that force is also the driver of creation and creativity, then I cannot deny the power of this force. For decades I have shared this connection with my students, and as they have worked with this concept, their creativity—and their connection to the divine—has consistently blossomed as well. Over the next seven days you will work with tools to discover this link for yourself, and explore what creative endeavors you might like to begin—or continue—with God's support.

CREATIVITY AND SPIRITUALITY

When I was newly sober, I worried that my creativity would disappear without the additive of alcohol. But my newly acquired sober friendships advised me that creativity and spirituality went hand in glove. And so, skeptical, I posted a little sign by my writing station. It read, "Okay, God, you take care of the quality. I'll take care of the quantity." With that dictum in mind, I began to write. To my surprise, my writing came easily, not at all resembling my previous ego-driven striving for cleverness. As page after page unfurled, I recognized that creativity and spirituality did indeed go together. From intellectually grounded short essays, my writing expanded to longer essays and then to entire books.

Before I got sober, I was always trying to be brilliant and impressive. After I got sober, I tried to write more from a spirit of service. When I did that, my writing became clearer and more accessible, and to my surprise and delight, my career took off. Creativity and spirituality were so connected that I considered them to be one and the same.

I have written this way for forty-plus books over forty-plus years. When I try to "take something down" rather than "think something up," words follow. I am receiving rather than trying to control. Letting a Higher Power write through me, I find I sit down to write with more ease. When I sit down to write, I find it best to start where I am.

Outside the window, fog envelops the piñon tree. Its flock of ravens has disappeared into the silvery mist. My courtyard glistens with new snow. My trainer's footprints from this afternoon are erased. Night falls through the fog, taking with it the shape of the mountains one more time drenched with snow. The cloud that came down from the heights, becoming fog, blurs the outline of the peaks it left behind.

Looking past the piñon tree to the mountains beyond, I am greeted by a thick silver cloud, caught on the summit. My friend Nick hikes the snowy peaks with sixty pounds of weight strapped to his back. He is in training for a marathon in March and I wonder, staring at the cloud, if he is able to navigate safely. He tells me that his marathon is named the Bataan Memorial Death March. It is being held in White Sands, New Mexico, on a missile range. He tells me he's been tinkering with a poem inspired by the mountains, that it has "some good things." He says, "I sat down to write, and I heard, 'write about the mountains.' I thought, 'How dumb.' But I obeyed."

I wished for what I always wish for.
I wished for another poem.

—LOUISE GLÜCK

Don't think or judge, just listen.

—SARAH DESSEN

Nick's "rough, rough draft" is the result. His writing, like his daily trek, is muscular. Sitting over tacos at The Red Enchilada, he shoves the poem across the table. "Here," he says. "For what it's worth. Read it later."

Back at home, alone, with Nick's mountains looming outside my window, I read his description of Moon, a small "feminine" mountain. He wrote, "She hides beneath prolific piñon like a dark green veil." My adobe house hides beneath my piñon tree, "a dark green veil" made darker still by the circling ravens, their great wings casting shadows on the tree below.

A poet as well as an athlete, he records, daily, the "mood of the mountain." Ever a perfectionist, he feels his words fall short of capturing his experience as he climbs. He writes, "Sun Mountain, old stone soldier, windswept and bare . . ." Reading his draft, I look to the mountains with fresh appreciation. "Connected by a sloping rocking bridge to his sister, Moon." She is "like a reclining lover. With her dress heaped over her hips."

Nick's poem is bold and erotic like the peaks he climbs, naming them as he hikes. He courts danger daily on the rocky heights. He tames that danger with language—and with prayer.

The silver cloud descends the flank of the mountain, bringing with it more snow. The flakes fall gently but quickly. The cloud, down from the high mountains, drapes itself as fog on my lesser peak.

As I write, I—like Nick—hope to capture something of nature's wild spirit. My piñon tree has sisters on the flank of Moon Mountain but it has a world of its own as well. It feeds ravens. It offers refuge to little birds. At its base, squirrels pick over the nuggets of nuts the birds left behind. I watch the tree bedecked with snow, then bare. Wind rifles its branches. Veils of snow drift gently down. The tree is both delicate and sturdy, made by its maker to withstand both cold and heat.

As artists, we, too, are both delicate and sturdy. Sometimes we feel our delicacy to be a liability. We wish for a thicker skin. And yet, as poet Julianna McCarthy says, "If we rid ourselves of our vulnerability, we rid ourselves of our capacity to create." And so we must be open to the pain that comes with life. Our openness moves us to create.

I pray, "Please, God, help me be open. Allow me to be of service." And then, "Thank you, God, for my piñon tree. It is beautiful." I am reminded that the piñon tree grows from the same source that allows me to put words to page. Through the green fuse . . .

◄ TRY THIS ►

All of us have a direct line to the divine. The Great Creator is interested in supporting our creative endeavors of all sizes—from redecorating the bathroom to shooting a feature film. Fill in the following sentences:

If I let the Great Creator create through me, I'd try . . .

If I let the Great Creator create through me, I'd try . . .

If I let the Great Creator create through me, I'd try . . .

If I let the Great Creator create through me, I'd try . . .

If I let the Great Creator create through me, I'd try . . .

If I let the Great Creator create through me, I'd make . . .

If I let the Great Creator create through me, I'd make . . .

If I let the Great Creator create through me, I'd make . . .

If I let the Great Creator create through me, I'd make . . .

If I let the Great Creator create through me, I'd make . . .

If it didn't feel so risky, I'd . . .

If it didn't feel so risky, I'd . . .

If it didn't feel so risky, I'd . . .

If it didn't feel so risky, I'd . . .

If it didn't feel so risky, I'd . . .

Now create a small sign: "Okay, God, you take care of the quality, I'll take care of the quantity." Post it where you create. Allow it to serve as a reminder of the connection between creativity and the divine.

BLOCKING AS AN ISSUE OF FAITH

Snow falls gently. According to the forecast, we will have only a light dusting. And so I look out the window toward the mountains and see them frosted with white. I am working on a play and each scene unfolds smoothly, but not without anxiety. I worry nightly that I will run out of ideas, even though my guidance assures me that I will not.

I have taught creative unblocking for decades, and no matter the type of artist—writer, composer, painter, filmmaker—the tools to remove blocks to higher and more free-flowing creativity are the same. At its core, blocking is an issue of faith. We worry that we won't have enough ideas or that our ideas won't be good enough. We worry that what we've said has already been said better by someone else. We make a film, write a book, compose a score—and worry that we can't do it again, because we "only have one in us." At the root of all of this is a lack of dependence on God to give us what we need: tools for the project, ideas, collaborators, even funding. None of these human concerns are out of God's reach. God has unlimited ideas, unlimited money, and unlimited help. We need only open the door to this help. When we allow ourselves to be open-minded and actively seek the support of our co-creator, we are able to move forward and create with more ease.

"You will write freely," I am told, and so I put pen to page, writing longhand, facing down my fear of an empty well. As the snow falls and I trust that it will indeed be a light dusting, I recognize that my faith in the weather and my faith in my creativity are both issues of trust. Blocking, I realize anew, is a matter of faith. It is not something to be understood and moved on from, but in fact an ongoing dialogue with God. As I take to the page daily, my faith is tested. I ask for help, and I move my hand across the page. Guidance tells me a scene will unfurl. My faith that I am well and carefully led increases as the pages of the play accumulate. Today I am at page eighty, and I trust that I must write "freely" until I reach a hundred and thirty handwritten pages, which will translate to a hundred pages typed.

Writing each scene as it comes to me, I am indeed being led forward to write a play that is both optimistic

You can't use up creativity. The more you use, the more you have.

—MAYA ANGELOU

and romantic. My working title for the play is *True Love*, and the drama centers on two loving couples who find themselves facing the future with courage and optimism. Each night as I put my pen to the page, I feel a surge of grace. If blocking is a matter of faith, unblocking, too, is a matter of faith. And so I write.

My characters talk to one another freely and humorously, as though they have no idea that faith is at stake. At this moment, I am consciously practicing faith about the reception of my plays in general. Guidance repeatedly tells me, "Both of your plays will find homes. You will be well pleased." Wanting the plays to be welcomed by good theaters, I find myself reading the guidance over to myself and thinking, "Maybe." Whenever I ask about the plays, the reassurance is the same. "Have patience," I am told and so I strive to have patience and— impatient—I doubt the good tidings I am told I'll receive. Having faith in my "bright" theatrical future requires that I have faith in God's timing and that faith is hard to come by.

Allowing myself to trust the guidance and continue work on my newest play, I feel my doubts receding. Creativity is always the answer. Allowing my anxieties about "my plays in general" to be channeled into the act of writing, I am given energy to write, and my anxiety retreats. I must allow a loving God to partner with me on all aspects of my plays, from creation to production. I need not push God away out of fear or distrust. Allowing the creator into my creation, I move forward with ease. One page at a time, I am led.

The storm outside the window shows signs of lessening as my writing moves toward the climax. I am tempted to put the storm into the play, and as I do so, I experience relief. My guidance is accurate. The play, indeed, should be called *True Love*.

Listen to your instincts and ignore everything else. Ignore logic, ignore the odds, ignore the complications, and just go for it.

—JUDITH MCNAUGHT

◄ **TRY THIS** ►

There are times in our lives when we feel we cannot trust God. We believe that God can't, or won't,
help us with our dreams and agendas. Perhaps we
assume our requests are too lowly, too selfish, or
too foolish. Perhaps we are mad at God, and like a
child fighting for independence, we want to "do it
ourself." Allowing yourself to resist your resistance,
fill in the following sentences:

I pushed God away when . . .

I pushed God away when . . .

I pushed God away when . . .

I pushed God away when . . .

I pushed God away when . . .

Now, look at your life in the present. Are there
any ways in which you could ask God for help now?

I suspect that I may be pushing God away in
regard to . . .

If I believed that God could help me, I would . . .

If it wasn't too frivolous, I would ask God to . . .

If it wasn't too crazy, I'd tell God . . .

The thing I most want God's help with today is . . .

THE NATURE OF PATIENCE

This morning I woke to a snowfall. Flakes pelted down. Already, half a foot of snow was on the ground. My plans for

the day had to be scuttled: God's will had me snowbound. The earth was hushed except for the raucous cawing of ravens as they flapped through the storm. I didn't take well to canceling my day's agenda. I had looked forward to a meal with Nick. When I called him to say I was snowbound, he said, "I thought I might be getting this call." Although I drive a four-wheel-drive Subaru, good sense dictated that I not brave my road, which goes unplowed. And so, with reluctance, I bowed to the storm. The quiet day might be good for writing, I realized, grumpy at the thought. When a huge raven soared past my window, I surrendered. Yes, there would be something to say, to write about after all.

My friend Julianna McCarthy lives on a mountaintop in California. She, too, had suffered an overnight snowfall, but she took her stormy weather with good grace. "I love the snow," she shared with me. "I love weather." Unlike me, she took the day in stride. "We've got a lot of snow," she exclaimed with excitement. Over the forty years of our friendship, I have marveled at her ability to take things—and weather—as they come. Tutored by a habit of morning prayer, she faces each day surrendered to its unfolding. She is patient—patient with God—and she seldom argues over the shape of the day at hand.

Just now, I am arguing. My meal with Nick has been postponed for days, and I am impatient with the delay. As if mocking my mood, the storm outside intensifies.

"Call me again if you feel trapped," Nick said, hanging up. I do feel trapped, just as he predicted. Lily ventures out into the storm. She comes back in a moment later, wet and wild. She is a West Highland Terrier, a small white breed, a snowball herself. She leaps to the back of a love seat, damp and chilled.

"Treats, Lily?" I ask her. She ignores me, staring out the window at the storm.

I phone my friend Scottie, who is basking in sunny San Diego, recuperating from bone graft surgery. "Hello,

Art washes away from the soul the dust of everyday life.

—PABLO PICASSO

Julia," Scottie answers her phone, muffled. I tell her of my highjacked day, and she ventures, "Maybe it's a good day to write. I'll light some incense." It is Scottie's habit to pray using incense. She believes that incense "takes prayers straight to the heavens."

"Please do light some incense," I tell her.

"I'm not in pain," she volunteers. "I'm healing."

I remark that her prayers are painkillers.

"Yes," she laughs. "I think so."

Getting off the phone, Scottie lights incense, and, prayed for, I put pen to page.

I pray daily for patience. Mine is an impatient nature. When I fight with God—and I do, and I lose—it is most often over the matter of timing. I want what I want and I want it *now*. When I question God about time, I hear back, "My timing is perfect. Trust it." And so I try to trust, observing the sun and moon in their flight, steadying the pace of God's seasons. Try as I try not to, I argue with the divine unfolding. Spring always comes too late, winter too soon. "What is God thinking?" I mutter to myself until, defeated, I pray my prayer for patience.

"Please, God," I ask, "give me patience." Faced as today with a long and empty day, I take to the page.

Writing a book, I find the pages accumulate slowly. When I try to flog myself forward, I meet resistance. Speed, it would seem, is not God's will. Awaiting news of my plays, I must practice patience daily. Must the theaters read so slowly? Yes, evidently they must. Mine, after all, are not the only plays they are considering. And so I wait for news, thinking that "new" is a misnomer. And when "news" comes, it comes with a personal note: "Thank you for your patience." If only they knew. But perhaps they do, and hence their kindly note.

I have a wish, and that is that God would send me a note. "Just hang in there," God's note would say. That, and "I sympathize." God's sympathy for my impatience would soothe me, I think. But then I reflect on the many times when God's timing has proved right in the end. After all, a belated spring proves itself all the more glorious, and the full moon, when it comes, proves itself, too, to have been worth the wait.

"You're building character," I have been told by an older and wiser friend when I protested some unseemly delay. "Damn character," I want to say, although I take pride in my character's tiny improvements. "There. You were patient," I told myself upon receipt of the theater's note. I puffed myself up just a little, vain on my own behalf.

Last night I talked to a New York friend, a medical doctor and psychotherapist. "With this book of yours, I think God is teaching you patience," she told me. "You write a paragraph at a time, praying to be led, and you are led, but only a paragraph at a time. You're impatient, and want to write more quickly, but the book will unfold one paragraph at a time. Patience: that's the lesson."

The creation of a thousand forests is in one acorn.

—RALPH WALDO EMERSON

After I talked with her, I took one more time to the page, writing not on the book, but on guidance. I asked to hear higher wisdom. That was my prayer. I listened, and wrote what I "heard."

"Little one, much good comes to you now. We understand your anger and impatience. You are eager for your artistry to be recognized. We ask you to trust us on your unfolding. We lead you carefully. Do not ask us to rush. Velocity is not the answer. You need to be grounded. We have much wisdom. Allow us to guide you."

And so, tutored by what I call "higher forces," I am able to—at least briefly—let go of my demand for speed. I am able to wait to hear about my plays, and I am able to accept that my book on prayer—this book—would best be served by a temperate pace. Just as the smoke from Scottie's incense drifts heavenward slowly, so, too, my thoughts on prayer would develop without untoward velocity.

I no sooner resolved to slow my pace than I had a phone call from my friend Suzanne, a high-powered New York realtor. I was accustomed to her voice sounding tense and pressured. Instead, she sounded . . . calm. "I'm meditating," she told me when I asked. "I'm making malas—prayer beads. And I have a mantra that I use. I meditate for twenty minutes using my prayer beads. I think it's really helping me." I told Suzanne she sounded relaxed and she told me I sounded "good."

"I'm writing a book on prayer," I told her.

"Maybe that's why you sound good to me," she replied, her new voice light and joyous.

With my nose pressed to the window, I can just make out the piñon tree, branches laden. Its silhouette is lumpen. Surely it must stop snowing soon, although we have five hours remaining on the snow-stops-at-midnight prediction. I am eager for a blue day, with the snow sparkling in the light. I am eager to drive out and see people—people!—my day at home has been lonely. This, despite calls to break my solitude.

"I prayed for you today," Ezra calls to tell me. I count myself lucky to be on the receiving end of his focused prayers. "Tomorrow, I'll pray for your writing," he promises, and I look forward to his support. "I want to hear more!" he exclaims when I read him a snippet of what I've been writing. Knowing that he will pray, I know there will be "more."

Actress Jennifer Bassey calls from sunny southern Florida. Her warmly theatrical voice is reassuring. She prays throughout her day, and her prayers temper her volatile nature. She sounds sweet.

"I pray all day, seeking to have conscious contact throughout—not just praying first thing in the morning and then going on my merry way," Jennifer volunteers.

"I ask for patience," she explains, "because by nature I am impatient. I ask myself constantly, 'What would God do in this situation?' Then I strive to be loving, because I believe you get back what you send out. This morning, I got a phone call saying, 'I hate people. They're terrible.' I responded to my caller, 'Be careful what you say and send out, because that is what will come back to you.' When I send out love, I get love back. I receive everything I need."

I tell Jennifer of my impatience with my plays, of my impatience with the storm, and my abandoned plans to go out. She sympathizes. "I try for acceptance. This morning I got impatient because a little old man in front of me was driving very slowly and I was late. I was tempted to honk, but then I remembered acceptance. 'Let him drive slowly,' I thought to myself, and I did.

"As often as I can, I pray during my day," Jennifer goes on. "I pray prayers of healing and prayers to get over my resentments. I'm telling you, it works. I receive answered prayers. I strive daily to be more Godlike, and little by little I improve." Jennifer snorts with laughter. She confesses, "I've still got a long way to go."

Nightfall comes, and still the ravens brave the storm. It is dark, but the birds are darker, inky black against the glowering sky. The storm is unrelenting. The big black birds zoom above my piñon tree. They glisten in flight. I wonder if the bold birds enjoy the snow. They have not taken to shelter, and so they must.

The natural world surrenders gracefully to the storm. The chamisa bushes—bright gold in autumn—turn silvery beneath the snow. The piñon tree dips its branches, heavily laden with frigid weight. In the garden, berries glow bright orange against the white.

Safe inside my snug adobe house, I am bundled in pajamas and a robe. The furnace labors mightily, spewing warm air against the chill. It's now pitch black, and little Lily is restless. She stares out the ebony windows, sensing the storm but not seeing it. At last, she stretches full-length on the love seat. Like me, she is mustering patience to wait out the storm.

The painter has the Universe in his mind and hands.

—LEONARDO DA VINCI

◄ TRY THIS ►

We are all, sometimes, impatient. Sometimes it is with ourselves. Sometimes it is with other people. Sometimes it is with God. At the core of impatience is fear—fear that we won't get enough, that we won't get what we deserve soon enough or often enough. We can use love for our inner artist to cure its fear. Quickly fill in the following sentences:

If it wasn't too late, I'd try . . .

If it wasn't too late, I'd try . . .

If it wasn't too late, I'd try . . .

If it wasn't too late, I'd try . . .

If it wasn't too late, I'd try . . .

If I had no fear, I'd make . . .

If I had no fear, I'd make . . .

If I had no fear, I'd make . . .

If I had no fear, I'd make . . .

If I had no fear, I'd make . . .

GODSENDS

There is nothing too small to ask for God's help with. As I have gotten into the habit of talking to God, I find myself asking for help with everything, from the large—"Please keep me healthy. Please let my writing be of service"—to the tiny: "What should I start with today?" or "Help me pack for my trip." I find that when I ask for help, I am likely to receive it.

"Your need is water and prayer," I am crisply informed when I ask for guidance after Morning Pages. I have a head cold, and I am concerned because I am flying to New York in a few days—a trip that entails two fights: one from Santa Fe to Dallas, one from Dallas to New York. Obedient to the guidance, I gulp down half a bottle of water. My prayer is "Please, God, let me feel better." I pack my suitcase, or at least I try to. I'm going to be gone two weeks, and my clothes and books and notebooks overflow my little suitcase. The zipper won't close.

Gerard phones in, checking on my welfare. I tell him my suitcase is too small and too worn out.

"Go get yourself another suitcase, a bigger one," Gerard advises.

"I don't know where to get one," I protest. But Gerard is right. I do need a bigger, better suitcase. Getting off the phone from him, I call Scottie for help. She is an expert shopper. To my dismay, I get her answering machine.

"I need to get a new suitcase," I record my message. "Do you know where I should go?" I put on my coat. I bundle up in a hat and scarf. I will drive across town to a department store that carries luggage. Hopefully they will have what I need. I am headed out the door when my phone rings. It is Scottie. She got my message.

"I do know where you should go," she says confidently. "There's a travel store where I've had good luck. You take Guadalupe past the basilica to Montezuma. Turn right, and then right again into a driveway. You park, and the shop is behind you, right next to On Your Feet, the shoe store. It's a little hole in the wall, but they are very good."

And so I head my trusty Subaru one more time down the mountain. I take Guadalupe to Montezuma. I go right, and right again. I park and spot the shoe store.

Sure enough, tucked behind it, I see a sign: Bon Voyage. Scottie's little travel store.

"I need a good suitcase, but without a lock," I tell the salesman. "I get paranoid about a lock, that I won't be able to get my bag open. So, do you have something? I travel a lot. I take clothes and books and medicines. I need compartments."

The salesman—named Joel, I learned—listened to my needs and then rolled out two suitcases. One of them suited my needs perfectly. It rolled easily on four wheels and had compartments for medicines, liquids, and books. Plus a large compartment for clothes.

"I'll take it," I told Joel, thinking gratefully of the ease I would have in packing.

"It has a lifetime guarantee," Joel relayed to me, ringing up the sale. "Anything goes wrong, just bring it back in."

I thanked him for his time and attention, satisfied with my purchase. Back at home, my packing went easily. I phoned Scottie to thank her for her guidance. I phoned Gerard and thanked him for his suggestion. Looking back over my guidance, I discovered the phrase, "I am the great organizer." The new suitcase was quite literally a "Godsend."

The next morning dawns dark and gray. The sun does not put in an appearance. Instead, clouds block the mountains and a few tiny flurries announce the arrival of snow. The flurries thicken, becoming flakes. Now the sky is white. This is snow indeed. The heavens shed flakes like tiny feathers.

The storm, for it is a storm, gathers velocity. A stiff wind blows the flakes sideways, whirling like petticoats. The piñon tree provides a shelter for little birds. They bob in and out of the snow-laden branches. In the distance, ravens cruise, riding out the wind.

By noon a thick blanket covers everything. Still the flakes fall. The dirt road is a sheet of white. I note an

My God was always there, but now I have learned to talk to him.

—ERIC CLAPTON

answered prayer: yesterday's head cold has all but disappeared. But I dismay at the stormy weather and the cancellation of yet another day's plans.

"I do understand," my friend Nick's friendly voice came over the line. "If you feel crazy later, give me a call."

I had complained of being one more time snowbound. He sympathized but told me the roads were "treacherous." He didn't urge me to try them, having once skidded into the ditch just outside my house.

Everything you can imagine is real.

—PABLO PICASSO

"You're a writer," he said now. "That gives you another world to go to." A writer himself, Nick knew of what he spoke. He was busily at work on "new" poems, bringing his drafts to dinner with me on Thursdays. Over tamales and tacos at The Red Enchilada, he shared his verses— and his reservations. "This one's a little corny," he introduced last Thursday's poem. "Hush up," I told him. "Let me enjoy it without judgment." And then I read the poem to him aloud.

"They always sound better when you read them," he complained, as if reading his poem aloud was somehow "cheating."

Now he said, "I'm having an okay day. I can't complain." I could hear him pulling his mood up by his bootstraps. I thought of my daughter's comment about not being alone and I realized that Nick's understanding of my nature was a gift from the Higher Power. Nick told me that my understanding of his nature was also a godsend.

Hanging up the phone, I caught myself thinking, "Godsend." What a literal term.

I believe that we come into each other's lives as blessings. How else to explain the mysterious chemistry that connects us across rooms and across continents? My friendship with Nick began when he was newly arrived in Santa Fe. At dinner, on our first meeting, he told me of his habit of early morning writing and prayer. After writing, he sat quiet, practicing one of several forms of meditation. I told him his practice sounded like my own, although I never practiced formal meditation. By just sitting quiet, just writing, I found I got my guidance on the page. Nick didn't correct me. He wore his spirituality lightly, although soon after he shared with me his definition of prayer: "focused goodwill." I liked it and I liked Nick, thirty-six years my junior, but wise for his years. Yes, he was a godsend. God sent us into each other's lives.

As I write, my friend Jacob is preparing dinner in Boise, Idaho. Andrew is sleeping in London. Sonia is waking up early in Paris. I am connected to each of them through prayer: focused goodwill. Night has fallen now, and with it, more snow. The little dog ventured out and came back in haloed in snow. She dipped her muzzle into her water bowl to defrost it. From Seattle, where her musical *Bliss* is getting on its feet, Emma calls me.

"Let me check the weather," she says and a moment later warns me, "It's going to be cold in Santa Fe, twenty-eight degrees tomorrow, so the ice won't melt. Call someone to check before you go out driving."

I think to myself Emma is another godsend, cautioning me to be self-loving, not impatient. I think of the patience she has practiced for years in developing her musical together with her partner Tyler Beattie. They have inched ahead, perfecting their craft and now they are on countdown for opening night. If Emma could be patient for years, surely I could manage another day. I pray for Emma and her show. She prays for me and my impatient temperament. The web of prayer connects us both.

I phone Jacob, who is just finishing dinner. "I prayed for your writing," he tells me, listening expectantly for my report.

"It worked," I report. If prayer is focused goodwill, Jacob's goodwill is palpable. Another godsend. His prayers reach me across the miles.

Writing out my Morning Pages, I asked for guidance. I was told, "Have curiosity about what God will bring you." And so I am curious why my phone rings and it is an unrecognized number.

"Julia, it's David Samora," my caller says. "How are you?"

"I'm claustrophobic," I announce dramatically. "I'm snowbound."

"I'm not claustrophobic," David replies. "I've been out and about all day. I'm used to snow. I'm practiced at driving in it. If you're claustrophobic tomorrow, I'll come over and take you out to dinner."

"Oh, thank you, David, but I have an interview on prayer scheduled for six o'clock. It's over at The Red Enchilada."

"Will you be able to get there?"

"I don't know."

"I'll tell you what. I'll come pick you up and drive you. Be ready at five fifteen."

"I don't know." I was nervous at driving and nervous at accepting help. David laughed gently. He was calm, steady, and persuasive. Still I balked.

"There's a ditch by my driveway. You have to back out." Was I trying to scare him?

"I remember. I helped someone—Nick?—get out of a ditch at one of your dinner parties. You're nervous. Just say, 'Thank you. I accept.'"

And so I swallowed and said, "Thank you. I accept."

"Good," David said. "Now if you'd say a prayer for me, I have to give a speech tomorrow morning."

"I pray for wisdom, humor, and grace," I told him.

"That's what I'll pray for, then," he chuckled. "See you at five fifteen."

And with that I thought: curious and curiouser. Yet another godsend.

Unfold your own myth.

—RUMI

> ◄ **TRY THIS** ►
>
> As artists, we need "Believing Mirrors" in our lives—those who mirror us back to ourselves as large, competent, and exciting. Our big dreams sound right-sized to them. They assume we can achieve them because they believe in us. One of our chief needs as creative beings is support—and support, when we find it, is truly a godsend.
>
> List five Godsends in your life, past or present:
>
> 1.
>
> 2.
>
> 3.
>
> 4.
>
> 5.
>
> Choose one person from the list. Can you reach out to them now and thank them for their help? Can you be inspired by them to be a godsend for someone else?

THE LIGHT OF ENLIGHTENMENT

In my nearly forty years of teaching creative unblocking, I have often said that "enlightenment" is a quite literal term. From the front of the room, I see faces brighten, steps lighten, and spirits lift as my students work through the tools of recovering their creativity. Again, the connection is not lost on me. As people work on their creativity, they work on their spirituality. As they learn to "lighten up" through the play of Artist Dates, they find themselves more productive, more open, and more—yes—enlightened.

Tonight I am giving a speech, and I am nervous, as I always am before I teach. I have learned that in the moment of teaching, I am always guided, led idea to idea, sharing with the room what I am "told" they need to hear. My guidance has never failed me. Still, I remain apprehensive before the talk begins. I pray to be of service, and I ask friends to pray for me.

I have two deceased friends who prayed for me when I taught: Jane Cecil and Elberta Honstein. Their prayers took on the coloration of their personalities. Jane, an actress, wished me humor and charisma. Elberta, a champion horsewoman, brought forth stamina and poise. Jane has been "gone" four years now, and Elberta three. I still ask them to pray for me, and I still feel their unique support. It is my belief that prayer, like the soul, thrives in the afterlife. When I ask for help with my writing, I ask both the living and the dead. If prayer is focused good wishes, I enjoy help from both sides of the veil.

It's morning now, but the sun doesn't shine. Instead, the sky is overcast, threatening further snow. The ravens are once again busy, hurdling through the air, swooping and soaring, dive-bombing my piñon tree. A particularly bold and large bird perches atop a neighboring juniper, shaking loose the snow. A second, smaller bird joins it, and together they flap their wings in simulated flight. It strikes me once again that they are playing. The storm has made of their habitat a giant playground. What's this? A huge flock of dozens of birds swoops near my windows. Are they preening? Perhaps so.

The ringing phone breaks my reverie. The caller is my friend Scottie, lolling on her patio with her two small dogs, who, like her, enjoy the warmth of San Diego.

"I'm doing well. I'm healing. My spirits are good," Scottie reports of her post-surgery recuperation. "Shall I light incense for you?" she offers. I have told her that I am giving a speech tonight at six and I am nervous.

"Yes, that would be great," I tell her of the incense. Prayers, especially prayers for my nerves, are always welcome.

Outside my windows, the mountains have taken on rainbow hues. The sunset in the west is reflected in the

It is of great importance, when we begin to practice prayer, not to let ourselves be frightened by our own thoughts.

—SANTA TERESA OF ÁVILA

east. "It's beautiful here now," I tell Scottie, but she goes me one up.

"The boats in the harbor are lovely, and it's warm here," she gloats. I tell her of the ravens' antics, and she chuckles. "Enjoy the beauty of Santa Fe," she signs off. "I'm looking at palm trees."

It's seven fifteen and I have made my speech. Floating on Scottie's incense, I spoke of what else? Prayer. To an audience of strangers I find myself speaking of written prayer, prayers from the dead, and the power of prayer to transform lives. Case in point: mine.

Talking about the power of prayer, I watched my audience closely. They were alert and attentive, hunched forward in anticipation of what I might say next. When I opened the floor for comments, they were eager to share.

"My day goes smoothly when I pray," a listener volunteered. "When my day is bumpy, I realize, 'Oh my God, I forgot to pray.'"

"I pray when I first wake up," volunteered another. "It sets the tone for my day. I ask God to guide me, and throughout my day, I check in to be certain I'm still on track."

"I forget to pray," a third person anted up. "Maybe that's why my life is such a mess."

As the comments ranged around the room, one woman spoke up tearfully. "I haven't been praying. I've been fighting with God. My brother died October fifth, a brutal, horrific death. I've been shaking my fist at God—'How could you let this happen?'" Telling the room of her grief, the woman's face softened. The room, and God, could accept her sorrow. Her tear-stained face was itself a prayer. Voicing her anger had helped her. She might, now, even pray.

A hunch is creativity trying to tell you something.

—FRANK CAPRA

TOWERING ABOVE THE crowd of diners at Love Yourself Cafe, Steve Jimenez picked his way to a corner table and took a seat. Well over six feet tall, wearing a red plaid shirt, blue jeans, and boots, he was casual but imposing. His shaved head gave him an air of majesty. He could have stepped from the cast of *The King and I*, good-humored and charismatic. A writer and filmmaker, he took a break from his creative endeavors to talk about prayer.

"Yes," he said. "I prayed as a child. I had a grand-mother who was deeply spiritual and she was a strong influence. And, too, I was sent to Catholic school—from first grade, for eight years. Religion was taught in school. Further, I was an altar boy, rising daily at five thirty to serve mass, walking the five blocks to church, come hell or high water."

Jimenez smiled, recalling himself as a bright, imaginative child immersed in ritual and mystery. "As a boy, I was enchanted by Francis of Assisi. His story became a touchstone of my spirituality—simple and direct, in contact with nature.

"My childhood God was of a benevolent male authority. But then so many of the figures were female—Mary, Mary Magdalene—that my deity became not exclusively male."

This was a departure from conventional Catholicism, and Steve's curiosity led him still further afield. "The period of the late sixties and early seventies was a time of exploration of spirituality for me. All different kinds of eastern philosophy and mysticism—Hinduism, Buddhism."

Untethered from his roots, Steve found himself in crisis. His parents were divorcing, and his world felt unsettled. A freshman in college, he was anxious and adrift. Almost miraculously, he met a mentor—a distinguished Jesuit priest, Tom King, S. J., who took him under his wing.

"He gave me guidance and counseling. He was a really devout mystic who had a deep practice of the Christian mystics—John of the Cross, Teresa of Ávila. Under his wing I healed. The basic steps of prayer that he taught me are still with me today."

Steve's meal arrived and he forked up a mouthful. "Delicious," he pronounced it. He continued, "He taught of divine madness, of the saints and the sages. In many traditions, the precept is to silence the noise in your mind—to disconnect. Instead he said to 'enter the madness,' that it was an essential step to not deny where you are. He had a pretty wonderful sense of humor. He made it seem safe to be vulnerable. I began a daily practice: enter the madness, then enter the silence."

Steve sipped at a cup of tea. "I began to realize how much resistance I had to life as I found it. I began to accept life as it was. Instead of rushing ahead into the day, I slowed down. I found that by slowing down I was far more productive and creative."

And so Steve has led an active life, plunging into his film work, pausing only to write a book, *The Book of Matt.* His personal spirituality has deepened and expanded as he himself has become enlightened—coming to see he was intended to be free. One symbol of his freedom is his shaved head. When I ask him about it, he tells me, "I've been shaving it for twenty years now. To me it says I'm more open, cleaner. What you see is what you get."

NICK DEMOS SETTLED himself at his kitchen table. Outside the window, palm trees bobbed in the wind. It was a mild day in Los Angeles and he was dressed casually in blue jeans, black tennis shoes, a Henley T-shirt, and a light blue jacket. His gaze drifted to the garden. In silhouette he was a striking figure—shaved head, aquiline features, lean and fit from his yoga practice. Self-described as a "creative entrepreneur," he wears many hats: theater producer and director, yoga practitioner and instructor,

The chief enemy of creativity is good sense.

—PABLO PICASSO

writer, teacher. The list goes on. Resting his elbows on the table, he began.

"I was never taught to pray. My parents weren't religious, although they believed in the Golden Rule, 'Do unto others as you would have them do unto you.' There was a sense in the household that there was a greater Something, and I was fascinated by religion at a very young age—three, four, five. Our neighbors were Spanish speaking and went to a Spanish-speaking church, and I wanted to go with them. My parents let me go. I couldn't understand, but I enjoyed the ritual.

"As a very young person, I believed in God as a loving presence," Nick continued. "Then, as I grew older and tried to come to terms with my gay sexuality, God evolved into an angry and oppressive figure. Looking back, I see that when I was young, I prayed for things I didn't want—'Please don't let there be a test tomorrow,' 'Please don't let me be gay'—rather than praying for the good. At age sixteen, I ran away from God and called myself an atheist. I rejected a dogmatic God who had an issue with my sexuality."

Nick leaned forward, cupping his chin in his hands. He went on, "At age eighteen, I was in such pain, I opened up again to the idea of God. I became a seeker looking for a God who accepted all parts of me, less bound by rules, more bound to the concept of love. I began looking at New Age wisdom. I read every book I could find. Marianne Williamson, Gary Zukad, Louise Hay, Brian Weiss. The books led me to yoga."

"I now sit every day for forty minutes. And I absolutely have a connection to the divine. The reason for the practice is to let go of little things, to focus on the things and people who matter. Don't sweat the small stuff."

Nick gazed out his kitchen window to his garden. It provoked a further thought. "Over time, my God con-

"Hope" is the thing with feathers
That perches in the soul
And sings the tune without the words
And never stops at all.

—EMILY DICKINSON

cept became more Buddhist. I've heard it said, 'Prayer is talking to God; meditation is listening to God.' I've become more interested in listening."

Nick made a steeple with his fingers. He continued, "In my twenties, I was seeking, but I was confused. Now, I'm forty-eight. I am a practitioner and instructor of Hatha yoga. I've been teaching for fifteen years. My artist has grown from my practice."

I found my God in music and the arts.

—ERIC CLAPTON

Nick's artist is indeed large. I have worked with him for several years perfecting a beloved play, *The Animal in the Trees*. A complex and difficult play examining both alcoholism and manic depression, it is to Nick's credit that he is able to be both delicate and bold. Sympathetic to the characters, he requested changes that made them both more vulnerable and more lovable. Making my changes in the directions he indicated, I found myself feeling he was true to both the play and my voice.

Nick summed up his relationship to his Higher Power: "I'd say my prayer life now is conversational. No formal prayers, but a technique called 'Metta.' I recite, 'May Julia be safe, happy, peaceful, free.' I don't say it aloud. I say it all in my head."

"And that shaved head. Is it a mark of humility?"

Nick laughed again. "Not a mark of humility. A mark of vanity. I was going bald." His laughter deepens and is contagious. He exemplifies "enlightenment means 'to lighten up.'"

◄ **TRY THIS** ►

One of the quickest ways to find a lightness of heart is to pamper ourselves. We think that being hard on ourselves will make us strong, but the opposite is true. Treating yourself like a precious object will make you strong.

List five ways—large or small—that you could pamper yourself this week:

I could pamper myself by buying two containers of raspberries at the market.

I could pamper myself by buying a new set of sheets.

I could pamper myself by giving myself a day of "no expectations"—taking the pressure off to achieve anything.

I could pamper myself by . . .

I could pamper myself by . . .

ASKING FOR PRAYERS

It's a clear blue day. Most of the snow has melted, and the piñon tree has dropped its blanket. Lily is perched on the back of the love seat, staring out at a flock of ravens wheeling in the sky. Mine is a peaceful household, save when the phone rings. The caller is Jacob Nordby, who wants me to know he's saying prayers for my prayer book. I tell him I'm grateful. The daily prayers of my friends get me over my resistance at taking to the page. Scottie tells me she is lighting two special sticks of incense that I might write freely. Faced with the page, I feel the support.

"Prayer is real," my friend Julianna tells me. Her belief is palpable.

"Pray for my writing," I ask her.

"Of course. Always," she replies, and I find myself wondering how much of my productivity I owe to her prayers.

However, it's to my friend Nick that I owe a working definition of prayer. "Prayer is focused goodwill," he tells me. When I ask him to pray, I feel his goodwill.

Everybody who is human has something to express.

—BRENDA UELAND

As artists, we can ask God for help and support with our art, and we can also ask for help from our friends. I have made it a habit to ask friends to pray for my writing—and I am always happily willing to pray for theirs. As we find those kindred spirits with whom we can safely share our art, we are behooved to explore and pursue these relationships with openness and honesty. Artists love other artists. As we support and listen to each other, our art flourishes.

Scottie calls, and I tell her her incense is working: I have pen to page. "I won't disturb you, then," she announces. "Let's talk in a couple of hours." I picture her seated on her patio in sunny San Diego. At her side, two sticks of incense send their fragrant smoke wafting heavenward.

"I've been lighting incense for thirty years now," Scottie has told me. "People know that's how I pray. I will get a phone call where the caller says, 'Here's my intention; light some incense for me.'"

"So I'm not the only one," I think, "who asks Scottie for prayers." Judging by my own case, I deem her prayers most effective. The incense, like my ravens, takes wings to the sky, bearing good tidings. Prayers for writing result in writing. I write, as Scottie's pre-dawn request, "with ease and joy."

Now a bank of snow clouds is moving in over the mountains. A few flurries set the ravens into hijinks. Wheeling close to my windows, they balance atop the portal, tails bobbing in the wind. Their good humor is contagious. "Thank you, God," I pray, tickled by my private air show.

Now the snow clouds blot out the mountains. The ravens call to each other, saying, perhaps, "Come play." The bold leaders land on the piñon trees' uppermost branches. One huge bird peers directly into my living room.

"Hello, you," I breathe. I am reminded again of the raven as "the first animal," a harbinger of good tidings. Settled again atop the love seat, Lily swivels her head, ears perked, attentive to the ravens' cries. She is curious, and perhaps a little frightened. The giant birds are nearly her size. If they are bringing good tidings, Lily needs a translator. There is a break in the clouds, and sunlight suddenly dapples the landscape. The ravens settle, waiting for more flurries to stir them into flight.

My phone rang: a welcome late-night call from Jacob Nordby.

"I've been thinking about you and your prayer book," Jacob led off, his voice a low rumble.

"Yes?" I said, eager to hear his thoughts. We regularly prayed for each other's art. He was himself finishing a book, a book called *The Creative Cure*. I thought he might have some valuable tips for me. Instead, to my dismay, he offered me the by-now familiar advice: "Slow down."

He explained, "I had to write my book twice, because I had to live it. I think you may have to live your book."

Just how would I "live" my book, I wondered? I certainly dreaded writing it twice. And wasn't I already living it? I prayed for guidance daily. I wrote as I was guided to write. The very topic—"prayer"—had come to me when I asked for guidance on what to write next. I heard a single word: "prayer." I asked:

LJ: What about a prayer book?

I was told: "Little One, you have chosen well. There is much to be said about prayer and you can say it. You are led carefully and well. This topic is a good one, and you are a good writer. Do not doubt your subject. It is worthwhile . . . ask us for help and we will give it to you. Trust us to guide you. We will give you ideas and a flow of words."

If you ask me what I came to do in this world, I, an artist, will answer you: I am here to live out loud.

—ÉMILE ZOLA

"A flow of words." That is what I needed to hear—not "slow down." I pictured a river. I dip my pen into its current, and then I write. Jacob's call was brief; it was, after all, late. I took myself to bed with snow pending.

It's two days later, and snow still blocks my drive. I edge my car gingerly through a drift and onto the still-icy roadway. I head down the mountain, grateful to reach a paved road that has been plowed. I worry that after my errands are run I will not be able to make it back up.

"I worry when I should pray," it occurs to me. "Please keep me safe," I petition. I am talking to God, and to all higher forces. Still nervous, but less worried, I drive on.

My friend Gerard has phoned me daily as I waited out the storm. On his last call, he advised me to stay in at night.

"Wait for daylight to drive," he advised me gravely.

Heading back up the mountain in late afternoon, I decide to heed Gerard's advice. Errands run, I'm ready for safety. I pilot my car carefully into my drive, edging it into the garage. Safe! I greet little Lily at the doorway. She is relieved to have me home. I wonder if the ravens have put on a show for her in my absence. Lily isn't saying.

So now I am curled on my love seat with Lily stretched out beside me. "Please keep me safe," I remember my prayer, and I feel a surge of gratitude. The snug adobe house does hold safety for both the little dog and me. I am settling in for a quiet evening at home writing when my phone rings. It's Jacob Nordby, ordinarily a welcome call.

"I should tell him," I think, "that I resented his advice to slow down."

"Julia," Jacob greets me urgently. "How are you? I've been a little worried." He does sound concerned. We haven't talked in several days, unusual for us. I draw a deep breath, reassuring him that I am fine. And then I plunge awkwardly on, telling him my feeling that he was over the line, telling me to slow down, to "live my book."

"Oh, goodness," he responds, taken aback. "That wasn't my intention. I'd never presume to tell you how to write. I was relating my own experience."

"And how to pray, too," I interject. "I felt when you said I had to 'live' my book that you were saying I needed to have a fuller experience of prayer."

"Oh, no, goodness, no!" Jacob exclaims, alarmed, clearly shaken. "I'm so glad you're telling me this. I try to never dictate to anyone, even to my students, how to pray. There are so many different ways."

"Well," I say, "now I've told you. Do I sound defensive?"

"If something doesn't sit right, always tell me," Jacob urges. "I value honesty in our friendship. Is there anything else?"

"No, that was it," I answer, relieved to have cleared the air.

"Good," Jacob breathes. "I so value our friendship." I can hear his vulnerability, and so I tell him, carefully, "My guidance tells me we are kindred spirits, that I am secure in your affections, and that great good comes of our connection."

"All of that is true," Jacob says, relief palpable in his voice. "It's snowing here now," he adds. I wish him safety, glad that our friendship is restored.

Properly understood and applied, [prayer] is the most potent instrument of action.

—MAHATMA GANDHI

◄ TRY THIS ►

When we find artists with whom we can share our early ideas, we can consider these connections an answered prayer. It is important to be discerning when we choose the people who we share our

(cont'd)

"brainchildren" with, and it is important to be honest when we run into a bump on the road with those who we cherish. Fill in the following:

A person I can safely share my ideas with is . . .

A person I think I shouldn't share my ideas with is . . .

A person who might be overly critical is . . .

A person who might try to control my ideas is . . .

A person who I need to be honest with is . . .

A person who I could ask for prayers about my art is . . .

A person who I could offer prayers for their art is . . .

A person I trusted but shouldn't have is . . .

A person I think I should give another chance is . . .

The person I most value prayers from is . . .

BLISS

I am in the back of a limousine, driving from Santa Fe to the Albuquerque airport. The drive takes about an hour and fifteen minutes. It is a scenic ride through desolate, striking terrain. The highway acknowledges the vast emptiness by setting a high, seventy-five miles-per-hour speed limit. And yet, cars whiz past going eighty and ninety, hurrying across the unpopulated land.

My driver is Hector, a calm and helpful man. He drives steadily at seventy-five, two hands on the wheel. My prayers for safe travel are answered by his even pace.

I am headed to Seattle where I will teach a workshop—an exciting event. Some two hundred souls are attending. I will teach Saturday, ten to four thirty, and then—after a light supper—I will attend *Bliss*, a world premier musical written by my colleagues Emma Lively and Tyler Beattie. To date, the show has been seen by twenty thousand people and has garnered from them nightly standing ovations. I am eager to see *Bliss*—the culmination of six years' work. Living in Santa Fe, not New York, I have followed the show's progress by telephone. Emma has reported in daily the spills and chills of casting, choreography, costumes, and sets. "I finally think it's solid," she reported recently, just before the first standing ovation. As the cheers have mounted, so have Emma and Tyler's hopes. Their dream is to bring the show into New York. My guidance has said, "*Bliss* is on track and Broadway bound." I'm excited to see Emma and her show.

Hector pulls into a rest stop at Santa Domingo Pueblo. "It's windy," he notes as the car is buffeted by a strong wind. I am worried. If the winds are too gusty to take off, my flight may be canceled. But as we head on the highway farther south, the winds die away. The airport is calm and I find the staff of Alaska Airlines to be friendly and helpful. Checked in, I make my way to my gate, stopping at Baskin-Robbins for a Cappuccino Blast—a coffee and ice cream concoction that keeps me occupied for the hour I must wait until my flight boards.

The flight from Albuquerque to Seattle is bumpy—the rogue winds buffet our regional jet. To distract myself from the turbulence, I speed through a stack of tabloids, learning the faux details of life in the fast lanes. At last,

Sometimes you must be afraid of big wishes, because they are likely to be realized one day!

—SKENDER NITAJ

safely landed, I am met at baggage claim by a driver who pilots the way through a maze of parking garages to a highway, and to my hotel, the Fairmont.

At the hotel, Emma is waiting to greet me. We'll go to dinner at the hotel's excellent seafood restaurant, Shucker's. I order king salmon with risotto and it is succulent. We have a day to rest before I teach.

The hotel has an excellent spa and gym, and I make the most of it in our free day. An early dinner back at Shucker's sends me to bed ready to get up early and write pages before I teach. As always, I am nervous, and I pick at my breakfast of oatmeal and berries. Emma and I rendezvous at nine for a 10 a.m. start. I will be teaching an intensive day, working through the primary tools of *The Artist's Way*.

At ten sharp, I start teaching. We begin the day by singing, and the class is on pitch and eager to begin. I ask for a show of hands for how many are doing Morning Pages. Half the class signals that they are. "Feel smug," I tell them, as I teach pages for the other half. I finish with questions and answers, a favorite part of the day. Students love having their curiosity satisfied "straight from the horse's mouth." Next, and for the remainder of the day, I move through tool by tool by tool. I find my students to be eager learners, good-humored and swift. At day's end I am rewarded with a standing ovation. The class is well-satisfied by what I have taught. I am satisfied as well. Seattle has proved itself to be hospitable.

And now it is time for a quick dinner—and *Bliss*. I am seated dead center in the orchestra, next to Nick Demos. He has traveled up from Los Angeles, eager to see the show. It opens with a rousing number by the show's delicious villain, played by Mario Cantone. High energy and innovative, it next reveals the central cast: four princesses who have been locked in a tower for ten years. Their yearning for freedom is the engine that drives the action.

Only those who attempt the absurd can achieve the impossible.

—ALBERT EINSTEIN

They are not conventional princesses; rather, they are idiosyncratic and highly educated, eager to make their way in the world at large. But can they find their "happily ever after" without conforming? The show answers this question with an emphatic "yes." "To thine own self be true" is the show's mantra. Bliss, after all, comes with authenticity. Comic but serious, the show unfolds with lavish sets and costumes. At show's end, the audience leaps to its feet. A standing ovation shows its appreciation of the message.

Have I said the show's music was wonderful? I retired for the night humming a particularly memorable number. My dreams were filled with *Bliss*.

◄ TRY THIS ►

Our dreams come from God, and God has the power to accomplish them. Fill in the following sentences:

If my dreams came from God, I would . . .

If God had the power to accomplish my dreams, I would . . .

If God was a benevolent co-creator, I would try . . .

A creative endeavor I would like God's support with is . . .

If my creativity came from God, I would like to . . .

FORTY-TWO YEARS TALKING TO GOD

Forty-two years—to the day—after that Wednesday morning in 1978, I am curled on a leather love seat in my living room. Across the room from me, on a small round table, sits a large and festive bouquet. It celebrates the anniversary of my sobriety—a date more significant to me than my natal birthday. The flowers are vivid and beautiful: wine-red roses, fuchsia carnations, fire-engine-red and orange lilies. Taken together, the blooms are a vibrant salute to a special day. Each flower has its unique beauty. They differ in tone but complement each other. Like the flowers in my garden, they are varied but lovely. As I sit to write, the flowers keep me company. They are a gift from Emma, a signal that she loves me and cherishes my sobriety. I am grateful for the luscious blooms, each one a prayer of gratitude. The flowers remind me to lift up my heart. "Thank you, God, thank you, Emma," I pray. My flowers pray alleluia.

My friend Scottie prays by lighting incense. Her prayers lift heavenward in the fragrant smoke. My friend Nick prays by hiking. He climbs a small mountain with sixty pounds on his back, anchoring him to the earth as he climbs toward the sky. My friend Laura prays making pots of homemade soup. My friend Suzanne prays with her fountain pen, delicate and bold, "so centering," she says.

Each of my friends, like each of my flowers, has a unique beauty. Each prays in a special, personal way. Just as God gave each bloom a special beauty, so, too, each of my friends has a particular voice. When we pray, we pray to a listening God, one with acute hearing that recognizes the unique timbre of each person who prays. God created thousands of flowers with particular care for each, great attention paid to detail. So, too, God pays attention to each of his human creatures, recognizing each face, each voice lifted in prayer. Listening to every being is a vital part of God's plan. The same patience, care, and meticulous attention God grants to the flowers, God grants to us. Never tiring of our diversity, God welcomes each of us. We, in turn, blossom in God's garden, a bouquet of souls.

Remember, no effort that we make to attain something beautiful is ever lost.

—HELEN KELLER

Speaking for myself, I have gone from being a tightly folded bud to a full flower. Over the years, my creativity has expanded. Working with the Great Creator in tandem, I have written a book a year. Each text is, for me, the proof that spirituality and creativity go hand in glove. As I have prayed to be led, I have been led. As I have asked for guidance, I have been guided. Row upon row of books grace my library, their leather-bound spines announcing that the Great Creator works through me. When asked how I have been able to be so productive, I pause, considering, and then answer, "I listen." As the universe unfurls a word at a time, I find myself marveling that I am an instrument. As I strive to be of service, I find myself fulfilled.

CHECK IN

How many days this week did you do your Morning Pages? Seven out of seven, we hope!

Did you take an Artist Date? What was it? Did you feel an increased connection to your Higher Power during the date? Afterward?

Did you take your walks? What insights bubbled to the fore?

Did you try asking for guidance in writing, and then listening to the answer? What guidance did you receive? Did you try applying it? What surprised you?

MARCHING FORTH, TALKING TO GOD

In this final week, we will experiment with the idea of God as a constant companion. There is no moment too large or too small to ask the Great Creator for help and support. I have found, for myself, that the more often I talk to God, the more often I hear from God. It is in talking to God that we are reminded, moment after moment, that God is with us always, ready to provide wisdom, protection, and inspiration. As we are willing to tap this unlimited and omnipresent resource, we are led, and led well. We march forth, talking to God.

THE POWER OF ROUTINE

Today was the first day that felt like spring. Temperatures were in the high fifties, and a light breeze stirred the piñon tree. The warmth in the air was tantalizing. This has been a long, cold winter filled with snow. An early spring would be more than welcome. My prayers for acceptance of the winter's chill could give way to prayers of petition. "Please, God, let it be an early spring."

But not yet. As nightfall darkens the evening sky, the air turns chill again. Winter is still with us. The last drifts of snow still burden the courtyard. Ice by the gate still makes the path to my door treacherous. Bundled in a sweater and blanket, I am curled on my love seat. The night is pitch black, and I turn to prayer.

Every night I get to my knees and say a prayer of gratitude for my sobriety. "Thank you, God, for my sobriety

What used to be the hunch or the occasional inspiration gradually becomes a working part of the mind.

—BILL WILSON

today." Then I cheat, and add another prayer: "Thank you for my sobriety tomorrow." The nightly prayer is a discipline I set for myself. Its regularity is a comfort and an exercise in humility. All prayer is good, but a regular practice of prayer is even better.

Throughout the centuries, the routines of the religious have marked the hours of the day and the days of the seasons. The discipline of their lives is a mark of their humility. Regular practitioners of prayer would no more go without it than breathing.

"Pray, pray, pray," says actor James Dybas, who has forty-two years on a spiritual path. He phones me to say hello, and our conversation turns to his daily practice of prayer. His actor's voice resonates across the miles.

"The first thing in the morning, when I open my eyes, I say, 'Good morning, God, it's me, James. I'm an alcoholic. Please keep me sober today. Talk to me and through me. Let me be of service. Thy will, not mine, be done.'"

Having forged his conscious contact, he slips from his bed to his knees, where he recites two more formal prayers. Then he looks out the window to the sky and gives a further prayer of gratitude for another sober day. Next, he prays aloud, his voice a deep rumble. "Help me to rely on you, God, deeply. Secure no matter what happens to me." He concludes his morning practice with a prayer for health. "God is, and I am, in radiant, vital, dynamic health." He offers this prayer three times.

Throughout the rest of his day, prayer is "an automatic, daily part of [his] life." He prays, if not constantly, consistently, at every step of his day.

And then at night, James one more time gets to his knees. He recites formal prayers, and then he prays "for the repose of the souls who have transitioned and for aid to the souls who are in special need."

Asked if he thinks regularity is an important part of prayer, he replies, "It's so important. Regularity and dis-

Supplication, worship, prayer are no superstition; they are acts more real than the acts of eating, drinking, sitting or walking. It is no exaggeration to say that they alone are real, all else is unreal.

—MAHATMA GANDHI

cipline are actually the most important parts of prayer." In his deep, theatrical voice, he repeats, "Pray, pray, pray—not just sporadically, but regularly. Prayer is so powerful—why go without it?" His question lingers on the air. Why, indeed, go without it? My clock ticks loudly, signaling the end of the day. Like Dybas, I turn to my nightly prayers.

◄ TRY THIS ►

You have now established four important routines: Morning Pages, Artist Dates, walks, and writing out guidance. Take a moment to reflect in writing about how these routines have affected your life. Are there other routines that you have naturally incorporated as you practice talking to God? Do you see an opportunity for further routine?

HOPE IS THE FLIP SIDE OF DESPAIR

It was a blue-sky day, although snow was predicted. Now clouds are rolling in—at twilight—and we may have some snow after all. My day was busy: a visit with Barbara McCandlish, a workout with my trainer Michele Warsa, a stint of thirty minutes on the treadmill. Now it is time to go meet friends and then, last but not least, I will write. I am balking at the task of writing. My "assigned" topic is despair and I have protested. Who wants to write about despair? Can't I write about something else? What about hope?

Hope is the flip side of despair. And so I look at the gray clouds rolling in and I *hope* it will not snow until I've done my rounds. If faith is a belief in a benevolent but unseen future, despair—hopelessness—is a belief in impending doom. Despair discounts the positive, dwelling on the negative and predicting more of it to come. To despair, there's no point *hoping* for a silver lining. To despair, depression is an appropriate reaction to life. When I find myself slipping into depression, I know that despair is just around the corner. Despair tells me I am alone, on my own without the aid and support of a Higher Power. If despair declares there is no God, or no God interested in me and my affairs, despair decrees the futility of prayer. Why reach out to a non-existent or at best disinterested God? Despair is a mask for discouragement. "What's the use?" it moans. In despair, there is no place for experimentation— "try prayer." Something worse than skepticism slams the door on spiritual matters. Contempt prior to investigation characterizes this stance.

For the despairing one, talk of God, a benevolent God, meets with contempt. God, if there is a God, is a fabrication of man's mind, a crutch for the weak, even a hoax. The despairing one points to the ills of the world—wars, genocide, famine—and pronounces, "What kind of god could allow all this?"

Blind to the good, the despairing one focuses on the bad with the expectation of the worse yet to come. Priding himself on his "realism," the despairing one refuses hope. Hope, he feels, is a delusion. If prayer is offered as a potent medicine, he denies himself its comfort. Calling his despair "rational," he fails to see that it robs him of potency. Believers, he claims, are naive. He refuses to be "gullible."

The despairing one denies God. If not actually and actively an atheist, he recites to himself proof of God's cruelty or indifference. Calling believers "childish," he declares his cynicism to be "adult." And who doesn't want to be adult? The despairing one clings to his skeptical intellect and denies his heart. And yet, put bluntly, the despairing one is heartbroken. Desolate and depressed, he is grief stricken. Abandoning God, he declares him-

Remember, hope is a good thing, maybe the best of things, and no good thing ever dies.

—STEPHEN KING

self abandoned. His woes are the woes of the world, he declares. He refuses hope and, hopeless, he refuses God and good.

The snow clouds threaten still, but I have hope no snow will fall overnight.

How wonderful it is that nobody need wait a single moment before starting to improve the world.

—ANNE FRANK

MORNING COMES, AND what's this? A flock of ten, twenty, thirty—more?—ravens cruises in for a landing beneath the piñon tree. They flap their mighty wings for balance as they pick their way carefully across the terrain, heads bobbing as they pluck up tasty piñon nuts. It is a festival of birds, sleek, black, and hungry. The boldest among them flap close to my windows. Their feathers glisten, striking. It is a clear blue day and the ravens take once again to the sky. They wheel in a great circle, then swoop back down, landing at the base of the piñon tree, resuming their lunch. Cued again of approaching danger, they rise back up, wheel in their circle, then soar down to peck up more treats. I watch all this from a sequestered window, marveling at the precision of their flights, their antics upon landing. I think to myself, "God will provide," as the ravens make their meal with plenty for all. What is hope, then, if not faith?

And what if we had the ravens' faith? What if we faced our times of scarcity certain that we would be provided for? My friend Nick, a fine writer, is in between writing jobs. I watch him demonstrate the ravens' faith, certain that "something will turn up." We eat dinner together every Thursday and Nick insists on paying "his fair share," refusing to hoard his pennies, trusting that a flow of cash will come. Like the ravens, he trusts God's bounty. He writes daily, doing his part, for love, not money. As the ravens fly because it is their nature, Nick writes because it is his nature. True to themselves—bird or bard—they trust in divine providence.

A hunch is your brain's way of taking a shortcut to the truth.

—CARLOS RUIZ ZAFÓN

My friend Laura, a retired school teacher, trusts that God will provide—but gives God a gentle nudge or two. She recently saw a sale on large-sized televisions, but her guidance said "Save your monies," and so she deferred. She laughs telling this story. She puts faith in her guidance as a guide to just how God will provide. She trusts that she will always have enough—provided that she listens carefully on when to save and when to spend.

Emma, a composer and writer, is frugal but daring. She spends modestly as a rule but she doesn't hesitate to spend lavishly on first-rate self-care. She sees a hairdresser regularly, invests in manicures, pedicures, and facials. She doesn't consider the gym membership a luxury. She believes in a God that wants her to have the very best.

I believe that faith and hope are intertwined. My friends demonstrate faith, while hoping for an abundant future. Like the ravens, they pluck their plenty from a generous and abundant universe. Believing God will provide, they are alert for proof of his care. Hoping always for a benevolent future, they spend with trust that their financial stores will be replenished. Alert to what they call "gifts from the universe," they believe, as I do, in synchronicity. Nick expects that he will have a paying writing job before his cash runs out. Laura scrimps on a fancy television but spends on a newfangled stock pot. Emma invests in a second pair of stylish glasses, one pair more than she needs, because they bring her joy. All three friends have faith that God will provide—and hope that the unseen future will prove to be ever more abundant. Like the ravens, chasing hope over despair, they are alert to God's bounty.

This week, buy yourself fresh flowers. Place them somewhere in your house where you will pass them often. Each time you pass them, you may wish to say a mental "thank you" for God's creativity and abundance. Allow the flowers to be a reminder of God's bounty.

> ◄ **TRY THIS** ►
>
> When we are alert to God's bounty, we are brought naturally from despair to hope. Fill in the following sentence ten times:
>
> I love . . .
> I love . . .
> I love . . .
> I love . . .
> I love . . .
> I love . . .
> I love . . .
> I love . . .
> I love . . .
> I most especially love . . .

PRAYING WITH—AND FOR—FRIENDS

It's a clear blue day. I can see the mountains and beyond, farther east to where an early three-quarter moon is rising.

"How lovely," my friend Laura Leddy exclaims. She is in Chicago where the moon's steady climb is blocked by buildings. "Is it a crescent, a quarter, a half?" she wants to know. She is removed from nature.

"It's three quarters," I tell her.

"Ah," she sighs.

Laura and I have been friends a quarter century. She knew me in my brief, ill-fated second marriage and she knew me afterward, heartbroken but resolute. I knew her through her long years of teaching and into her retirement. For a time, we lived in the same city, Chicago. Then our friendship survived my years in Manhattan and then the Southwest. We talk by phone at least once weekly and we support each other through thick and thin. Our chief means of support is prayer. We pray for each other's intentions and general well-being. Today, I ask Laura to pray for my writing, for ideas and a flow of words.

"That's easy," Laura says.

When Laura prays for me, I can feel it. A calm sense of strength fills my heart. I teach often, but never without "nerves." I ask Laura to pray that I may teach well, wisely and efficiently, with humor. Stepping in front of a class, I feel the steadiness of Laura's prayers. My nerves subside and I find myself teaching well, wisely and efficiently, with humor. I open the class to questions and answers.

"If you have some Qs, I'll try to have some As," I tell them. Hands shoot into the air. I pick one questioner, then another. The questions are sometimes difficult, but I find myself answering them with ease. Laura's prayers for me are being answered. I am relaxed and even funny. Amid the questions, I take a beat to pray myself. A flow of inspiration is my reward.

On today's phone call, I have an additional request. A cherished companion to my ninety-year-old friend Julianna has just been diagnosed with both leukemia and lung cancer. Doctors removed two thirds of a lung, cracking ribs to get to the site. Julianna has asked me for prayers and I, in turn, ask Laura. Over the years, I've come to trust Laura's prayers.

"What is her name?" Laura asks.

"Lisa," I answer.

"Lisa," Laura repeats, her voice already prayerful, steady, calm, and firm. Lisa will benefit. I am certain.

In our many years of friendship, Laura has prayed me through many books. She is familiar with my writing jitters and prays readily and steadily for my creativity. As each book emerges from my pen, I owe a debt of gratitude to Laura. Without her help, I might have floundered.

Embrace and open up your love, your joy, your truth, and most especially your heart.

—JIM HENSON

In addition to her prayers for creativity, Laura offers up prayers for health. At seventy-one, I enjoy robust health. Another answered prayer.

In return for Laura's prayers, I offer prayers. I ask for Laura to have "all good things," "all blessings," and "everything she needs." When Laura has a special intention, I pray for that, too. Her brother Tommy, deceased now three years, holds a place on my prayer list. Laura tells me she is grateful for my prayers. While I am certain hers are "better," I accept her thanks.

As the years pass, Laura and I pass them praying. Sometimes our prayers are formal—"masterminding"—and sometimes our prayers are more casual. "Please help Laura," "Please help Julia," we pray, trusting that God knows what is in our hearts. Our love for each other is steady, surviving time and distance. Our prayers for each other are the strong rope binding us together.

FRIENDSHIP IS HOLDING goodwill for another and goodwill is one definition of prayer. Over the years I have collected my friends carefully and I nightly remember them in my prayers. There is, of course, Laura. I pray for her health and general well-being. There is Scottie, who rises to pray every morning at three thirty and who receives my prayers later in the day. Nick and Jacob, believers in "focused goodwill," answer my requests for prayer with good-humored fervor. I, in turn, pray for them to "have all good things," "all blessings, everything they need." Ditto is my prayer for Jennifer, who believes in "white lighting" those for whom she prays. Julie prays "always," sending her requests heavenward, expecting a kindly response. My friend Gerard, a pragmatist, prays to God—good, orderly direction—ever sane and sensible. My friend Suzanne prays for particulars, blessings for herself and her family, and for me. I regularly ask for prayers from my two deceased friends, Jane Cecil

May the dark remain in your shadow and the light shine upon you.

—GIOVANNIE DE SADELEER

and Elberta Honstein. Through the ethers they assure me they're "on the case."

When I write out my prayers—near daily—they take up two full pages. As I write the names of my friends, I pray for them to have joy, health, peace, and acceptance, "all good things." Naming each one, I call them to mind fondly. I pray for the living and the dead, knowing we are all held by a loving God. I pray for those I know personally and for some I don't know. Sam Shepard—met, not known, but admired—comes in for regular prayer. Tom Meehan—another estimable artist—also enters my list. I pray for my doctors, for my accountant, Scott Bercu, for anyone and everyone whose goodwill matches my own.

"Your prayers are answered," my guidance assures me. "They are long ago heard." I trust my list of friends into the hands of my Higher Power. "I care for them all tenderly," I am told. Living in Santa Fe, far from many of my friends, I employ prayer to have a sense of connection. Asking God to remember—and bless—everyone I love, I experience the joy of that love. As my prayers reach outward, they also reach in. I experience the grace of answered prayer. My "focused goodwill" blesses others and myself. There is a formal prayer that I use frequently. A phrase in it goes, "relieve me of the bondage of self." That is the reward of prayer.

◄ TRY THIS ►

It is rewarding and inspiring to pray with—and for—our friends. Fill in the following:

Friends I could pray with are:

1.

2.

3.

Friends I could pray for are:

1.

2.

3.

Try praying with one friend and for one friend.
What do you notice about the experience?

MARCH FORTH

It's my birthday. I have always loved that my birthday,
March fourth, is also a command: "March forth." And
as I march forth, talking to God, I reflect on the path
my life has taken, partnered by God, and the gifts I have
received at every turn. I'm at Love Yourself Cafe, and
I've ordered oatmeal, fancy oatmeal made with coconut
whipped cream and maple syrup. When I tell Michael and
Hannah, the waiters, that it is my birthday, they volunteer
that I can be the recipient of a free dessert. Yummy, but
not for breakfast.

My day began early, with a spam phone call. It was
followed by another spam call, and then by a flurry of
calls from birthday well-wishers. There was a knock at my
door, and a festive floral delivery arrived. The bouquet
was vibrant: orange, scarlet, and fuchsia—New Mexico
colors that I love. I placed the arrangement on my dining
room table, boldly visible. The card was signed "Emma
and Tyler," so I phone Emma to say, "Thank you! The
flowers have arrived."

"What colors?" Emma asked.

"Orange, scarlet, and fuchsia," I told her.

"Oh good, I was hoping so," she replied.

My day looms ahead: calm. I will have a birthday dinner
with my friend Nick. I will celebrate my age, seventy-two,

Go where your best prayers take you.

—FREDERICK BUECHNER

and the fact that my friend Gerard stresses that I am doing fine. He tells me that fifty out of my college graduating class of four hundred have died. We know more than a handful of the deceased. Our good health is a blessing, Gerard insists, that we often take for granted. "We're doing very well," he states.

My oatmeal arrives, and with it a French press pot of coffee. I savor the oatmeal, which is sprinkled with cinnamon and almonds. The cafe is emptying out. Breakfast hour is over. I place an additional order for a vegan casserole: the skillet. At seventy-two years, plus one day, I will eat it. A treat for the morrow.

I return home and sit quietly writing. The last snow in the courtyard has melted, drenching the garden, ready for spring. Soon the lilac bush will be blooming, arching over the gateway, scenting the air. Daffodils and tulips quickly follow. Finally roses and lilies. Scent as well as sight makes the garden beautiful. Like incense, the aroma of the blooms wafts in the air.

It has been a long winter, and a snowy one. The beauty of the snow now gives way to green. Banks of lupine replace snow drifts. Warm air replaces chill. The little dog ventures out more often, and for longer. The sunlight on my wooden deck is inviting to her. The pool of warmth entices her to relax, basking in the light.

The phone shrills, and when I answer it, the caller is a florist. "I'm at your gate. I have a delivery." I tell the florist to enter the courtyard, that I will meet her at the door. She comes bearing an ample basket of flowers: roses, lilies, carnations, and gardenias. They are a thoughtful gift from my literary agent, Susan Raihofer.

I set the flowers on a small, wrought-iron table in my living room. They are a basket full of spring, a few weeks early. Their blossoms scent the air. Their basket blocks a corner of my mountain view. "Thank you, God, thank you, Susan," I pray. It is good to be remembered.

The basket comes from Susan. The blossoms come from God.

The bell rings, and I am greeted with another floral delivery. Opening the box, I find sixty tulips: a luxurious array of springtime blooms. There is no card. Who could they be from? My publisher, Joel Fotinos, calls.

"Did you get the tulips?" he asks.

"I did. Very extravagant!" I suspected the overflowing box might have been Joel's doing.

Joel chuckles, delighted through the phone. For twenty years my publisher, dear friend, and muse, he has never let an opportunity pass to express his appreciation for our relationship. Joel is another godsend, I think to myself.

On my back deck, there is yet another bouquet, this one from my friend Jacob Nordby. Bringing it in, I feel babied and spoiled. My house is filled with flowers, all signaling love and happiness. My answering machine registers six new messages, all birthday greetings. I cannot remember another birthday as lavish as this one. Maybe, I think to myself, there's something good to be said about aging.

At dinner with Nick, I find my mood now less than buoyant. He is sympathetic. "Birthdays are something to be gotten through," he advises me. "At least that's how I have found them." Nick's compassion for my down mood takes the edge off of it. Flowers galore, I still find myself moody. "I'm beating myself up," I confess to Nick.

"Should have done more by this age?" he asks.

"Exactly." I marvel at Nick's ability to hit the nail on the head. My depression is the result of unmet expectations. What was good enough at seventy-one isn't good enough at seventy-two. I have unconsciously raised the bar. How unfair of me. Driving home up the mountain after dinner, I say a prayer for myself. "Help me, God, with this mood. Help me to get over my self-pity."

May you never become so cynical that you let a star fall without its wish.

—NICOLE LYONS

I come home to a phone call from my friend Jean-nette, a psychiatrist. Her voice is warm and soothing. There's no point in hiding my mood, and so I confess.

"Jeannette," I say, "I'm depressed. I'm full of self-pity. I'm surrounded by flowers from people who love me and I'm still depressed."

"Birthdays can be difficult," Jeannette counsels me. "They overturn schedules and upset plans. I'd say to accept your mood and know that it will pass. You do well to consciously count the positives. Positives dig you out of depression."

Thanking Jeannette for her advice, I resolved to count my positives and see my day's glass as half full rather than half empty. I tick off the positives: breakfast at Love Yourself Cafe. Writing by hand with a view of the mountain. Calls from friends. Dinner with Nick. And flowers—lots of flowers. My little dog curls by my side on the love seat. I stroke her silken coat. She nuzzles my hand. It is a good day after all. I will march forth.

Dwell on the beauty of life. Watch the stars, and see yourself running with them.

—MARCUS AURELIUS

◄   TRY THIS   ►

What if God's gifts for us were unlimited? (Hint: they are.) Fill in the following quickly, so as not to overthink your answers:

If God's gifts were unlimited, I'd try . . .

If God's gifts were unlimited, I'd try . . .

If God's gifts were unlimited, I'd try . . .

If God's gifts were unlimited, I'd try . . .

If God's gifts were unlimited, I'd try . . .

A FOUR-DEER DAY

Driving up the mountain toward home, I spotted four deer. They tiptoed across the pavement, then plunged into the underbrush. They were fat and healthy, not at all afraid of the approaching car. For my part, I was glad to see them. They are beautiful animals, plentiful but elusive. Spotting them always lifts my heart. It is unusual, seeing four. They usually travel in threes: husband, wife, and child. The four that crossed the road defy convention. The leader stops and swivels his great white ears, alert for the safety of his posse. Satisfied that all are safely across the road, he journeys onward. The others meekly follow.

Today is a gray day, snow pending. The mountains are one more time erased. Snow is already falling on the peaks. I have fetched a casserole from Love Yourself Cafe just in case tonight is too snowy to drive out. I stare out the window, past my piñon tree, watching as the storm moves closer. I find the snow disheartening. This winter has already been long and snowy. I, and everyone I talk to, is ready for spring.

Inside the house, spring is happening. My birthday flowers bloom on tabletops. They are holding up splendidly at a week and counting. Looking at them, I feel cherished. This was a bountiful birthday. My baskets of flowers tell me that I may live alone, but I am not forgotten. Tulips, lilies, roses—all are festive. All speak of God's abundance.

Now the storm has reached my windows. Tiny, biting flakes announce winter's determination to have a final word. The piñon tree captures a blanket of white. Once more, tiny birds take refuge. It is a day for prayer. "Dear God, please make the storm brief." But the heavens are clouded over and the storm pelts down.

I am hoping it will be clear enough by six for me to

Find magic in the little things, and the big things you always expected will start to show up.

—ISA ZAPATA

drive out and meet with friends. The storms creates a sense of isolation, and friendships are particularly welcome. This winter has been a lonely one. Frequent storms have blocked the roads, necessitating enforced solitude. Santa Fe is a mountainous town, and here at the upper altitudes the snowfall is dense. Down in the heart of town, a thousand feet lower, the snowfall is typically lesser. And so, when I head down the mountain an hour from now, the storm will be less fierce.

"God, please keep me safe," I pray, and I feel a sense of calm. The great creator heeds my prayer by lessening the storm. Is it just coincidence? I think it's vanity to expect my tiny prayer to affect the weather. More likely, my prayer affects me. The sense of calm is internal, not external. Whichever the case, I will take it.

For tonight, when I return from seeing friends, I have two phone calls to make. The first is to Emma. She is reading this book, and I am eager to hear her progress and her opinion. The second call goes out to Jeannette. The storm makes me edgy and she is a steadying influence. A check-in with her focusing on positives typically finds me feeling calmer. Both calls cut my feeling of isolation. I report to them both: a four-deer day. Hooray! I tell them both of my lucky sighting. A four-deer day is auspicious. From my publisher, Joel Fotinos, I receive a welcome note: "Happy you got the flowers. We lifted a glass to you on your birthday." When I talk to Emma, she confirms, "We did lift a glass to you."

May God make your wishes come true.

—LAILAH GIFTY AKITA

As I CLOSE out this book, weathering one last storm, I am glad to hear a report of Emma's progress. "Dear God, please let the book be okay," I pray. And as I put my final sentence to the page, I feel assured that it is. A four-deer day, after all. A book on prayer is a "worthy" undertaking, and now it's done.

CHECK IN

How many days this week did you do your Morning Pages? Seven out of seven, we hope!

Did you take an Artist Date? What was it? Did you feel an increased connection to your Higher Power during the date? Afterward?

Did you take your walks? What insights bubbled to the fore?

Did you try asking for guidance in writing, and then listening to the answer? What guidance did you receive? Did you try applying it? What surprised you?

ACKNOWLEDGMENTS

Jennifer Bassey, for passion

Tyler Beattie, for witness

Judy Collins, for example

Joel Fotinos, muse

Domenica Frenzel, for far-seeing

Gerard Hackett, for loyalty

Nick Kapustinsky, for versatility

Laura Leddy, for faith

Emma Lively, for inspiration

Jacob Nordby, for insight

Scottie Pierce, for vision

Susan Raihofer, for clarity

Ed Towle, for wisdom

INDEX

ABOUT THE AUTHOR

© Robert Stivers

Hailed by *The New York Times* as "The Queen of Change," **JULIA CAMERON** is credited with starting a movement in 1992 that has brought creativity into the mainstream conversation—in the arts, in business, and in everyday life. She is the bestselling author of more than forty books, fiction and nonfiction, as well as a poet, songwriter, filmmaker, and playwright. Commonly referred to as "The Godmother" or "High Priestess" of creativity, Cameron considers herself "the floor sample of her own toolkit" because her tools are based in practice, not theory. *The Artist's Way* has been translated into forty languages and sold more than five million copies to date.